Evan Hendricks, a native of Portland, Oregon, is editor/publisher of *Privacy Times*, a Washington-based bi-weekly newsletter that covers privacy and freedom of information law. A graduate of Columbia University, Hendricks is author of *Former Secrets*, a compilation of five hundred examples of valuable data the public has obtained under the Freedom of Information Act. Mr. Hendricks is past president of the American Society of Access Professionals. He lectures regularly on information policy issues.

Trudy Hayden is formerly director of the Privacy Project of the American Civil Liberties Union and author of the ACLU "Privacy Report," director of research for the New York State Commission on the Family Court Act, and consultant on privacy to the New York Civil Liberties Union. She is currently manager of Program Development and Foundation Relations for the New York Public Library.

Jack D. Novik served for ten years as a staff counsel and then as acting legal director at the American Civil Liberties Union. During this period he was counsel to the ACLU Foundation's Project on Privacy and Data Collection in which capacity he litigated many intelligence issues. He was coauthor of "Litigation under the Federal Freedom of Information Act and Privacy Acts." In 1986 he became executive director of the New York City Criminal Justice Agency.

Also in this series

YOUR RIGHT TO PRIVACY

A BASIC GUIDE TO LEGAL RIGHTS IN AN INFORMATION SOCIETY

SECOND EDITION
Completely Revised and Up-to-Date

Evan Hendricks
Trudy Hayden
Jack D. Novik

General Editor of the Handbook Series:
Norman Dorsen, President, ACLU

SOUTHERN ILLINOIS UNIVERSITY PRESS
CARBONDALE AND EDWARDSVILLE

93 92 91 90   4 3 2 1

Library of Congress Cataloging-in-Publication Data

Hendricks, Evan.
   Your right to privacy: a basic guide to legal rights in an
information society / Evan Hendricks, Trudy Hayden, Jack D. Novik.
—2nd ed., completely rev. and up-to-date.
      p. cm.—(An American Civil Liberties Union handbook)
   Rev. ed. of: Your rights to privacy / Trudy Hayden. ©1980.
   Includes bibliographical references.
   1. Privacy, Right of—United States. I. Hayden, Trudy.
II. Novik, Jack. III. Hayden, Trudy. Your rights to privacy.
IV. Title. V. Series.
KF1262.Z9H37   1990
342.73'0858—dc20
[347.302858]   89-21844
ISBN 0-8093-1632-3   CIP

The paper used in this publication meets the minimum requirements
of American National Standard for Information Sciences—Permanence
of Paper for Printed Library Materials, ANSI Z39.48-1984. ∞

Contents

Preface

This guide sets forth your rights under present law and offers suggestions on how they can be protected. It is one of a continuing series of handbooks published in cooperation with the American Civil Liberties Union (ACLU).

Surrounding these publications is the hope that Americans, informed of their rights, will be encouraged to exercise them. Through their exercise, rights are given life. If they are rarely used, they may be forgotten and violations may become routine.

This guide offers no assurances that your rights will be respected. The laws may change and, in some of the subjects covered in these pages, they change quite rapidly. An effort has been made to note those parts of the law where movement is taking place but it is not always possible to predict accurately when the law *will* change.

Even if the laws remain the same, their interpretations by courts and administrative officials often vary. In a federal system such as ours, there is a built-in problem since state and federal law differ, not to speak of the confusion between states. In addition, there are wide variations in the ways in which particular courts and administrative officials will interpret the same law at any given moment.

If you encounter what you consider to be a specific abuse of your rights, you should seek legal assistance. There are a number of agencies that may help you, among them ACLU affiliate offices, but bear in mind that the ACLU is a limited-purpose organization. In many communities, there are federally funded legal service offices that provide assistance to persons who cannot afford the costs of legal representation. In general, the rights that the ACLU defends are freedom of inquiry and expression; due process of law; equal protection of the laws; and privacy. The authors in this series have discussed other rights (even though they sometimes fall outside ACLU's usual concern) in order to provide as much guidance as possible.

These books have been planned as guides for the people

directly affected: therefore the question-and-answer format. (In some areas there are more detailed works available for "experts.") These guides seek to raise the major issues and inform the nonspecialist of the basic law on the subject. The authors of these books are themselves specialists who understand the need for information at "street level."

If you encounter a specific legal problem in an area discussed in one of these handbooks, show the book to your attorney. Of course, he will not be able to rely exclusively on the handbook to provide you with adequate representation. But if your attorney hasn't had a great deal of experience in the specific area, the handbook can provide helpful suggestions on how to proceed.

Norman Dorsen, President
American Civil Liberties Union

The principal purpose of this handbook, as well as others in this series, is to inform individuals of their legal rights. The authors from time to time suggest what the law should be, but their personal views are not necessarily those of the ACLU. For the ACLU's position on the issues discussed in this handbook, the reader should write to Public Education Department, ACLU, 132 West 43d Street, New York, N.Y. 10036.

Acknowledgments

The first edition of this book was greatly aided by Aryeh Neier and John Shattuck, then executive director of the ACLU and director of the ACLU's Washington office, respectively. They closely read the manuscript and made many useful suggestions. Lisa Grapek provided valuable research assistance on state privacy laws.

The second edition has benefitted considerably from the energetic research of Jesse Wing, a former member of the ACLU's Washington staff; from the contributions of Raquel Gomez and Diane Davidson to the production of the book; and from the guidance of Janlori Goldman and Jerry Berman of the ACLU Privacy and Technology Project.

The authors gratefully observe that Morton Halperin, Jerry Berman, Janlori Goldman, Allan Adler, Wade Henderson and the entire ACLU Washington office have done a remarkable job fighting for our legal right to privacy and are largely responsible for much of the "good news" that the reader will find in this book. The "bad news" in this field would be worse were it not for their efforts.

Jack Novik, coauthor of the first edition and a pioneer in developing the law of privacy, died in 1988. He is greatly missed by all who knew him.

Finally, Evan Hendricks thanks his loving wife, Rosario, their wonderful families, and Daniel for their support and inspiration.

Introduction

Privacy can mean many things to many people. Some associate the term with the right to abortion. Others think of the right to choose a sexual preference. Many simply consider it "the right to be left alone" in any number of contexts. This book does not cover those notions of privacy. Instead, it focuses on information privacy, which involves the legal rights of individuals in relation to information about them that is circulating throughout society.

The importance of information privacy has increased with the advent of the computer age and the information society. Like other phrases that describe the environment in which we live, these terms also have many meanings. One significant reality is that modern life has been transformed from an age when a handful of institutions kept a few paper records in filing cabinets into the fast-moving present in which so many of our activities are recorded and stored by huge computer systems operated by megacorporations and government agencies.

In many respects, all this takes place according to our wishes. People prefer the convenience of credit cards; they demand services from government; they need insurance. These and other modern necessities in turn require corresponding data collection and storage. That in itself is a dramatic change from precomputer times. Equally astonishing is the way institutions can send information at the speed of light, swap it with others, match lists, and manipulate data to reveal people's personal habits.

Data banks are sprouting up everywhere and data literally are zipping in all directions. A knowledgeable and skilled person with access to the right data banks can follow your most important activities—without ever laying eyes on you! This is not intended to startle you. But it provides a backdrop against which discussions of privacy must take place.

Many of the data networks are seen as a benign response to societal demands for faster service and greater efficiency —at least in terms of the way in which they've been operated to the present. Nevertheless, information is power. The advent of the computer age—control of personal data by large institutions and the leverage this provides over individuals—clashes with the American tradition of privacy and often with desirable limits on institutional intrusion into private lives.

As individuals, we all have an intuitive sense of territory which we try to protect against intruders. While these boundaries differ, it is widely accepted that matters of the home, as well as traditional family relationships such as husband-wife and professional ones such as doctor-patient or lawyer-client deserve maximum levels of confidentiality. The desire to safeguard individual autonomy and to protect traditional relationships against government intrusion gave rise to early notions of the American right to privacy. A brief review of history shows how those notions were reflected in the Constitution and then evolved to incorporate the informational right of privacy once we entered the computer age.

Although the importance of privacy is deeply ingrained in our political and social heritage, the right of privacy is not explicitly mentioned in the Constitution. But the Bill of Rights is, by its very nature, a broad affirmation of personal privacy because it limits the government's power to interfere with individual liberty. The free speech and free exercise of religion provisions of the First Amendment assure the privacy of personal beliefs and associations; the Fourth Amendment protects "persons, houses, papers, and effects" from unreasonable search and seizure; and the Fifth Amendment protection against self-incrimination restrains the government from coercing an individual to breach his or her own privacy. But the development of privacy as a working legal concept has not equaled its importance as an article of faith. The law of privacy had suffered a grudging and hesitant birth and its growth has been stunted by the entrenched resistance of opposing interests.

In part, the problem is that privacy is not a single concept but a loose amalgam of different interests difficult to combine in one formulation. The Fourth Amendment prohibition against unreasonable searches and seizures, for example, was described by Justice Brandeis as the constitutional expression of the "right to be let alone."[1] The privacy protection in the First Amendment suggests personal autonomy, focusing not on what the government can do, but rather on the individual's freedom to be. Another important aspect of privacy is the right to exercise some measure of "control over information about oneself."[2]

The emergence of a distinct body of law dealing with privacy is generally credited to an influential law review article written by Samuel Warren and Louis Brandeis in 1890.[3] The right to privacy that they advocated concentrated on an individual's interest in preventing the commercialization of private matters by the press. Thereafter, in cautious increments, courts and legislatures first accepted, and then defined and enforced, a number of different principles which were described generally as a "right to privacy."[4] Intrusions on privacy were recognized as a civil wrong—in legal parlance, a tort. In some jurisdictions, it is improper for a person to publicize certain private facts about another without consent. A closely related tort is casting another in a bad public light by disseminating information reflecting an undesirable and erroneous public image of that person. Physical intrusion into a person's home or solitude, such as by eavesdropping, is also now often recognized as a tort.

The right to privacy, then, was initially interpreted to include only protection against tangible intrusions resulting in measurable injury. Courts were accustomed to thinking in those terms and took longer to address the more difficult issues of personal autonomy and information control.

During the first half of the twentieth century, the Supreme Court began to explore constitutional principles relating to privacy. In 1923, the Supreme Court invalidated a state law prohibiting the teaching of a language other than English because it interfered with personal autonomy: "The right of the individual to contract, to engage in any of the common occupations of life, to acquire useful knowledge, to marry, to establish a home and bring up children, to worship God according to the dictates of . . . conscience, and, generally, to enjoy those privileges long recognized as essential to the orderly pursuit of happiness by free men. . . ."[5] Similarly, recognizing that "the fundamental theory of liberty . . .

excludes any general power of the state" to compel standardization, the Court struck down a law requiring all children to attend public schools.[6]

In a 1958 decision that combined a recognition of the values of personal autonomy and information control, as well as First Amendment associational privacy, the court refused to allow a state to compel the disclosure of organizational membership lists. The decision articulated the "right of the members to pursue their lawful private interest privately and to associate freely with others" without "the deterrent effect . . . which disclosure of membership lists is likely to have."[7]

In 1965, in *Griswold v. Connecticut*, the Supreme Court for the first time held that the Constitution protected a right of sexual privacy. The case involved a Connecticut statute prohibiting married couples from using contraceptives. Justice William O. Douglas, writing for the Court, said the specific guarantees of the Bill of Rights created "zones of privacy" within a "penumbra." The First Amendment, he said, gave people the right of associational privacy and a certain degree of personal autonomy in their decisions. The Fourth Amendment affirms the "right" of the people to be secure in their persons, houses, papers, and effects against unreasonable searches and seizures. The Fifth Amendment's Self-Incrimination Clause enables citizens to create a zone of privacy that government may not force them to surrender to their detriment. Previous cases "bear witness that the right of privacy which presses for recognition here is a legitimate one." The Court found that the concerns of the marital relationship are within the zone of privacy created by several fundamental constitutional guarantees, and that a state, by forbidding the use of contraceptives, impermissibly intruded on that relationship.[8] A few years later the Court expanded this theme by striking down a law that limited access to contraceptives by unmarried couples. "If the right of privacy means anything, it is the right of the individual, married or single to be free from unwanted governmental intrusions into matters so fundamentally affecting a person as the decision whether to bear or beget a child."[9]

In 1967, in *Katz v. United States*, the Court applied privacy principles to a new sphere. It ruled that warrantless wiretapping was unconstitutional and in the process created a standard, known as "the reasonable expectation of privacy," to guide subsequent consideration of the issue. The Court set forth criteria for determining constitutionally protected "zones of privacy" — whether the expectation of privacy in the area to be searched outweighs the government's interest in searching the area, factoring the degree of intrusion involved. *Katz* and other cases suggested an interpretation of the Fourth Amendment and the Bill of Rights as a whole that provided constitutional protection not only to tangible property but also to an individual's communications, personality, politics, and thoughts.

In 1973, *Roe v. Wade* ruled that the Fourteenth Amendment was broad enough to include a woman's right to choose to have an abortion,[10] a ruling that has become symbolic of the right to privacy while remaining highly controversial.

A marked shift came in 1974 when banks and the ACLU challenged the Bank Secrecy Act's requirement that banks maintain copies of customer records for up to six years and give authorities virtually unlimited access to them to help fight money laundering. The Court held that the law's domestic recordkeeping requirements did not deprive the banks of due process by imposing heavy burdens on them; and the Court did not render unconstitutional the banks' government agents conducting surveillance on customers.[11] In a prophetic dissent, Justice Douglas challenged the law's recordkeeping solution to the problem of white collar crime, asking where this approach would stop. "It would be highly useful to governmental espionage to have like reports from all our bookstores, all our hardware and retail stores, all our drugstores. These records too might be 'useful' in criminal investigations."[12] Justice Douglas went on to say,

A mandatory recording of all telephone conversations would be better than the recording of checks under the Bank Secrecy Act, if Big Brother is to have his way. . . . In a sense a person is defined by the checks he writes. By examining them the agents get to know his doctors, lawyers, creditors, political allies, social connections, religious affiliation, educational interests, the papers and magazines he reads and so on ad infinitum. These are all tied to one's Social Security number; and now that we have the data banks, these other items will enrich that storehouse and make it possible for a bureaucrat—by pushing one button—to get in an instant the names of the 190 million Americans who are subversives or potential and likely candidates.[13]

The restrictive trend crystallized in a 1976 decision famous (or notorious) among privacy advocates but little publicized beyond them. In *U.S. v. Miller*,[14] the Court held (five to three) that the Constitution did not give individuals a right to privacy in their bank records. Instead, the Court reasoned, people surrendered their privacy when they opened a bank account because they handed over recordkeeping to a third party. The records thus were part of the flow of commerce and belonged to the bank, not the customer. The case arose when police sought bank files during a criminal investigation. The target of the investigation protested, stating that his constitutional right to privacy barred such access by the authorities without legal process. But the Court ruled that it was the bank's decision, not his, how records would be disclosed. The Court said:

> The [bank] checks are not confidential communications but negotiable instruments to be used in commercial transactions . . . [containing] only information voluntarily conveyed to the banks and exposed to their employees in their ordinary course of business. The lack of any legitimate expectation of privacy concerning the information kept in bank records was assumed by Congress in enacting the Bank Secrecy Act. . . . The depositor takes the risk in revealing his affairs to another, that the information will be conveyed by that person to the Government. This Court has held repeatedly that the Fourth Amendment does not prohibit the obtaining of information revealed to a third party and conveyed by him to Government authorities, even if the information is revealed on the assumption that it will be used only for a limited purpose and the confidence placed in the third party will not be betrayed.[15]

Miller became a flagship decision as the Court in subsequent cases applied its reasoning to other forms of personal records held by third parties. In *Smith v. Maryland*, a target in a criminal probe objected to the police getting his long distance toll records.[16] But the court held that the phone company could provide the information to the police without notifying the customer. In the medical area, the court in 1977 unanimously upheld a New York law requiring that copies of all prescriptions for narcotics be forwarded to the state for computerized storage.[17]

In sum, the Court sent out a clear message: if people wanted legal protection for all information that was being stored in institutional computers, they would have to turn to Congress, not the judiciary. Fortunately, three years previously, Congress had announced its intention to play an important role in shaping the nation's privacy policy by enacting the Privacy Act. This law applies only to federal agencies; it grants individuals the right to see, copy and correct their records and to restrict unconsented disclosures—both those occurring between different agencies and those outside the government.

During the legislative debate, Senator Sam Ervin and other congressional privacy advocates pushed hard for an omnibus law that would cover private sector records as well as federal government files. But President Ford said he would veto any such bill. As a compromise, it was agreed that the Privacy Act would cover federal files and that a commission would study the recordkeeping practices of employers, banks, hospitals, insurers, retailers and others and recommend to Congress what new protections were necessary.

Accordingly, Congress created the Privacy Protection Study Commission (PPSC), which met an ambitious two-year deadline and concluded that a national legislative program should be adopted. The commission, made up of an impressive array of congressional and presidential appointments and run by a capable staff, concluded that a range of new laws were required to shore up legal safeguards for personal records. The areas recommended for new coverage included medical, banking, insurance, credit, employment, and retail records.[18] The commission also concluded that the Privacy Act needed to be strengthened. While there were variations in the provisions recommended among different kinds of records, particularly for medical files, they rested on the so-

called Code of Fair Information Practices which formed the
core of the Privacy Act:

- The right to obtain a copy of one's record.
- The right to dispute or correct information that is
  believed to be inaccurate.
- The right to limit disclosures to outsiders who have not
  first received consent, and the right to know how one's
  personal information is used and who has access to it.
- The right to know what institutions and record systems
  contain personal information; i.e., there must be no
  personal record system whose existence is secret.
- Information obtained for one purpose may not be used
  or made available for another purpose without the
  individual's consent.
- An agency or organization that collects, maintains, uses
  or disseminates personally identifiable records is responsible for the timeliness, accuracy, completeness,
  and relevance of the records and for protecting against
  their improper use or legal disclosure.
- The right to legal recourse to enforce expectations of
  confidentiality.

Despite more than one hundred PPSC recommendations,
in the four years following release of the Privacy Commission's report, Congress passed only one law protecting financial records from informal governmental access. This was due
in part because, while the banking industry welcomed a law
that finally would define rules for financial privacy, other
interest groups opposed federal legislation in their areas.
Both the medical records bill and the insurance privacy
legislation received extensive consideration by Congress, but
neither was enacted. In addition, except in the area of financial records, Congress for the most part waited for the Carter
administration proposals. Intense debate within the administration delayed the Carter privacy policy until 1979, thus
limiting the time Congress had to consider it. The paucity of
results was all the more disappointing due to the high expectations raised by years of study and debate.

The Reagan administration never showed an interest in a
national privacy policy. Nonetheless, the importance of privacy and its acknowledgment by key lawmakers has led to

adoption of significant new legal protection. For instance, in 1984 Congress approved a law regulating cable television that included strong safeguards for customer files held by cable companies. In 1986 it enacted the Electronic Communications Privacy Act, a major revamping of the nation's wiretap laws in light of technological advances that made a 1968 statute obsolete. And in 1988 Congress passed legislation to regulate computer matching by federal agencies and a separate bill to protect the records of video rental stores from outside investigation.

The Supreme Court has continued its antiprivacy approach. In 1987 it acknowledged that public employees have a limited right of privacy in the workplace, particularly in desks and lockers to which other employees do not enjoy access. Nevertheless, it upheld a search in which state employees conducting an investigation of a hospital psychiatrist seized personal items from his desk.[10]

In 1988 the Court extended the 1976 *Miller* decision, holding that Americans do not have a constitutional right of privacy in their garbage. "Respondents exposed their garbage to the public sufficiently to defeat their claim to Fourth Amendment protection," said Justice White for a six to two majority. "It is common knowledge that plastic garbage bags left on or at the side of a public street are readily accessible to animals, children scavengers, snoops and other members of the public."[20] In dissent, Justice Brennan said the fact that burglars might enter private homes did not negate the right to privacy there. "Scrutiny of another's trash is contrary to commonly accepted notions of civilized behavior. I suspect therefore that members of our society will be shocked to learn that the Court, the ultimate guarantor of liberty, deems unreasonable our expectation that the aspects of our private lives that are concealed safely in a trash bag will not become public."[21]

Privacy has fared better in some states. Ten states have amended their constitutions to include an explicit right to privacy: Alaska, Arizona, California, Florida, Hawaii, Illinois, Louisiana, Montana, South Carolina, and Washington.[22] Moreover, the California Supreme Court has held that customers have an expectation of privacy in their bank and telephone records, and police can not obtain such files without legal process.[23] Similarly, in Colorado and Pennsylvania, two states that do not have privacy clauses in their constitutions, courts have held that government access to bank records amounts to a "search" requiring police to adhere to legal procedures.[24]

Unlike many European countries that have one law covering all kinds of personal information and a national commissioner to enforce it, there is a great deal of variety and inconsistency in the kinds of information and locations that are covered by privacy laws in the United States. Moreover, the United States does not have an official who oversees a national privacy policy. Such an official could, at a minimum, help individuals resolve complaints about record keeping and report to Congress what new legislation was necessary to preserve privacy rights in the face of rapidly advancing computer technology.

The concept of an individual's right to be free from unreasonable governmental intrusion is pivotal to all human rights. Opinion polls consistently have shown that Americans favor stronger privacy laws and are suspicious that large organizations use personal data for secondary purposes without their knowledge or consent. Many people view privacy laws as the individual's main defense against undue encroachment by large institutions—a sort of legal slingshot for fending off the computer-equipped goliaths dominating society.

The support of Americans for legal safeguards remains steady despite living under the influence of a variety of institutions that are hostile to privacy. Many large corporations have opposed legislation that would have bolstered privacy rights for customers and employees, viewing such proposals as nuisances rather than as steps to fundamental fairness. Yet they have not hesitated to cry foul when their own privacy was threatened. Government agencies continue collecting and sharing more and more personal data and have ignored provisions of the Privacy Act that were supposed to restrict such practices. Yet these agencies have complained loudly about their informants being compromised by Freedom of Information Act disclosures, just as corporations have charged that government procedures are inadequate to prevent release of their trade secrets to competitors. The major news media often treat privacy as a dirty word as well. While the press justly is outraged when bureaucrats frivolously invoke privacy to stop the public from learning valuable information, it nearly always rallies behind news reporters who are threatened with an order to disclose confidential sources. However, it also has been guilty of failing to focus attention on threats to legitimate privacy and of trampling upon the privacy of people who are not public figures but who happen to find themselves in the middle of a news story.

The process of protecting one's own privacy, of requesting or amending a record or otherwise controlling information about one's self, reflects a degree of participation that ought to be encouraged in a democracy. To resist or deter such participation or to deprive individuals of the opportunity altogether is wrong. A 1981 Congressional study put it well when in warned:

> The nature of societal values attached to privacy in the United States may change if larger and more ubiquitous information systems gradually remove the ability of individuals to hide their private activities.
>
> It has been pointed out that the possession by large organizations of personal data on individuals enhances the power, real or perceived of the organization over the person. These and similar effects may increase the suspicion some citizens have of large organizations—business, labor or government—and thus erode social cooperation and a personal sense of well-being."[25]

The concept of privacy is fundamental to the goal of fairness towards which democracies are supposed to strive. It is therefore crucial that reform of privacy laws be accelerated on the federal and state level so that rapid developments in computer technology do not strip individuals of the ability to maintain control over data about themselves that are circulating throughout society.

NOTES

1. *Olmstead v. United States*, 277 U.S. 438, 478 (1928) (Brandeis, J. dissenting).
2. A. Westin, *Privacy and Freedom* 32 (1967).

3. Warren and Brandeis, *The Right to Privacy*, 4 Harv. L. Rev. 193 (1890).
4. *See generally*, Prosser, *Law of Torts* 829 et seq. (3d ed. 1964).
5. *Meyer v. Nebraska*, 262 U.S. 390 (1923).
6. *Pierce v. Society of Sisters*, 268 U.S. 10 (1925).
7. *NAACP v. Alabama*, 357 U.S. 449, 466 (1958).
8. *Griswold v. Connecticut*, 381 U.S. 479 (1965).
9. *Eisenstadt v. Baird*, 405 U.S. 438 (1972).
10. *Roe v. Wade*, 410 U.S. 113 (1973).
11. *California Bankers Ass'n. v. Shultz*, 416 U.S. 21 (1974).
12. *Id.*
13. *Id.*
14. *U.S. v. Miller*, 425 U.S. 435 (1976).
15. *Id.*
16. *Smith v. Maryland*, 442 U.S. 735 (1979).
17. *Whalen v. Roe*, 429 U.S. 589 (1977).
18. Privacy Protection Study Commission, *Personal Privacy in an Information Society* (1976).
19. *O'Connor v. Ortega*, 480 U.S. 709, 719 (1987).
20. *California v. Greenwood*, 486 U.S. 35 (1988).
21. *Id.*
22. Alaska Const. art. I, § 22; Ariz. Const. art. II, § 8 (1982); Cal. Const. art. I, § 1, (1972); Fla. Const. art. I, § 23 (1980); Hawaii Const. art. I, § 6; Ill. Const. art. I, § 6, La. Const. art. I, § 5 (1975); Mont. Const. art. II, § 10.; S.C. Const. art. I, § 10 (1971); Wash. Const. art. I, § 7.
23. *Burrow v. Super. Ct. of San Bernadino County*, 529 P.2d 590, Cal. (1974).
24. *Commonwealth v. Goldhammer*, 469 A.2d 601 (Pa. Super. 1983); *People v. Timmons*, 690 P.2d 1274 (Colo. 1984).
25. Office of Technology Assessment, *Computer-Based National Information Systems* (1981).

PART 1
Collection, Access, and Control of Government Information

PART 1

I
Government Information Practices and the Privacy Act

Are there any limitations on the government's collection of data and information practices?

In theory, the Privacy Act of 1974,[1] enacted as part of the Watergate-era reforms, ~~regulates~~ virtually all government handling of personal data. In practice the Privacy Act is a weak and poorly enforced statute. Consequently, there are only minimal restrictions on federal agencies' collection, use, and disclosure of personal data.

What is the Privacy Act supposed to do?

The law was intended to set up a code of fair information practices between Americans and their government. It obligates agencies "to the greatest extent practical," to collect only "necessary" information directly from the individual. It also calls on agencies to inform people of the agency's authority to collect the data, of how it will be used, and of the consequences to the individual, if any, of not providing the data.

The law attempts to ensure that individuals are not haunted by wrong or misleading agency records by requiring that the government maintain all files with "such accuracy, relevance, timeliness and completeness as is reasonably necessary to assure fairness to the person." To preclude harassment of the government's political enemies, agencies are barred from maintaining records on how individuals exercised their First Amendment rights, except when authorized by statute or the individual or when pertinent to an authorized law enforcement activity.

Individuals have a right to see and copy their own records and to correct inaccurate information. However, intelligence and law enforcement agencies can exclude entire systems of records from individual access, though some of these records can be reached under the Freedom of Information Act.

To allay fears that giving information to one agency would be like giving it to the entire government, the act prohibits disclosures from one agency to another without the individual's written consent. The act lists, however, eleven exceptions to this restriction. The act provides damages for "willful or intentional" violations of the law. And finally, the act prohibits the maintenance of secret record systems (except by intelligence and law enforcement divisions) and requires agencies to publish a listing of their record systems.

Has the Privacy Act brought any benefits?

Yes. The Privacy Act has forced most agencies to pay at least minimal attention to records management and to observe basic protection for individual records. Because of the Privacy Act, individuals have the right to obtain copies of their records and correct inaccuracies, and thousands of people have done so. Agencies can no longer disclose records at the whim of a bureaucrat since there are penalties for abuse of personal data. But the act has not achieved its most important goal of assuring people that information about them collected by the government for one purpose will not later be used for other purposes. Instead, the public is in part justified in thinking that the government invades information privacy more than it protects it.[2]

Why hasn't the law achieved its goal?

There are many reasons. First, the principles upon which the act was based were diluted by exemptions. Second, no independent office was set up to oversee the law and assure compliance. Third, the courts, citing the many exemptions and vague language, often sided with the government against individuals in Privacy Act litigation. Courts also were hampered by the lack of provisions for injunctive relief and by the difficult standard for proof of an illegal practice. Fourth, agency officials took advantage of the act's vague language to carry out programs that at the least violated the spirit of the act. Let's first explore some of the court interpretations of the act and then show how the act's exemptions have given agencies wide leeway in their information practices.

A leading case stemmed from a secret government video-taping of a meeting at which Social Security appeals officers were informed that they would not receive promotions for which they had been recommended. There were a series of heated exchanges. When the appeals officers learned of the tape, they were sure it would be used to brand them "troublemakers" and claimed that this caused them emotional trauma. The court said the incident was unfortunate, but that the officers did not qualify for damages because they did not prove (1) the taping caused their emotional trauma and (2) the agency's violation of the act was "willful or intentional." A federal appeals panel in Washington said the "willful or intentional" standard did not include "all voluntary actions which might otherwise inadvertently contravene of the Act's strictures," but only those "when the agency acts in violation of the Act in a willful or intentional manner, either by committing the act without grounds for believing it to be lawful or by flagrantly disregarding others' rights under the Act." In other words, the appeals panel's interpretation made it more difficult for people to win damages under the Privacy Act.[3]

While winning damages under the Privacy Act is difficult, it also can be hard to amend records. In a complex 1987 case, the same court of appeals ruled that the Privacy Act did not always require agencies to determine whether adverse—and possibly inaccurate—information they maintain on individuals is true. The dispute arose when a State Department official claimed in a report that an applicant for a foreign service post admitted faking depression to obtain disability pay. The applicant (Jane Doe) learned of the report later because it caused her denial of a security clearance for another federal job. Ms. Doe provided extensive documentation to show she had had a medical condition, and moved to expunge the characterization, which she said was false. The State Department, refusing to delete the controversial statement, said it would only include Ms. Doe's version on the record.

The appeals court called the situation unusual, but said the Privacy Act did not require the State Department to decide whether its own official's assertions about Ms. Doe were true, only that records be maintained with "such accuracy and completeness as is necessary to assure fairness to the individual." In dissent, Judge Patricia Wald called the majority's ruling "fuzzy" and "untenable" and said she could find no warrant in the Privacy Act for dispensing with the duty to decide if the statement is accurate enough to be fair.[4]

How well has the executive branch implemented the act?
Generally, it has neglected it. For example, the Privacy Act
directs agencies to name a senior official to be responsible for
implementation. However, in a 1986 report, the General
Accounting Office (GAO) found that the Departments of
Education and Labor both had failed to put someone in
charge. The GAO identified seven Privacy Act duties: (1)
allowing individuals access to their records, (2) establishing
safeguards to prevent unauthorized disclosures, (3) setting up
periodic reviews of recordkeeping policies and practices, (4)
conducting training for government employees, (5) publishing notices of records systems, (6) maintaining Privacy Act
related procedures and directives and (7) reporting on and
monitoring agency participation in computer matching programs. In documenting widespread neglect of Privacy Act
duties, the GAO said that only the Departments of Defense,
Energy, and the Interior had assigned all seven functions to a
Privacy Act officer.[5]

Isn't some agency supposed to be in charge?
Yes. The Office of Management and Budget (OMB) is the
official overseer of the law. But a 1983 Congressional review
concluded,

> An [OMB] desk officer appears to have little if any
> responsibility to initiate an independent review of
> any aspect of an agency's information operations. This
> means that there is no monitoring by OMB of agency
> compliance with those provisions of the Privacy Act that
> are not reflected in the system reports. These provisions
> include such major features of the Act as the limitations
> in disclosure; accounting requirements, access and cor-
> rection procedures; notice requirements; information
> collection and maintenance limitations; and the require-
> ment for safeguarding information. Unless a problem
> with Privacy Act activities were reflected in a system
> notice, it is not likely that the problem would come to the
> attention of OMB. . . . OMB's oversight record for com-
> puter matching operations also leaves something to be
> desired.[6]

Perhaps the most significant damage that the executive branch has done to the Privacy Act is its interpretation of the "routine use" exemption, which opened the floodgates to widespread computer matching by many federal agencies.

What is the routine use exemption?

The Privacy Act aimed to preclude agencies from indiscriminately swapping data files by requiring that individuals consent to most disclosures. As mentioned earlier, the Act provided for eleven exemptions, including disclosures to Congress, the Census, the National Archives, criminal investigators, for health and safety emergencies, and for statistical research, or in response to court orders. The eleventh exemption was the routine use exemption which permits disclosures for "use of such record for a purpose which is compatible with the purpose for which it was collected." The idea was to give agencies some flexibility in making noncontroversial disclosures without obtaining each individual's consent when the purpose was compatible — but not necessarily identical — with the reason for the record's creation. Agencies must publish proposed routine uses in the *Federal Register* and consider any public comments prior to final adoption.

There are many examples of overly broad routine uses. The broadest is probably the Central Intelligence Agency's 1982 routine use to permit disclosure "to a federal, state or local agency, other appropriate entities or individuals, or, through established liaison channels, selected foreign governments whenever such disclosure is necessary or appropriate to enable the CIA to carry out its responsibilities under any federal statute, Executive order, national security directive or any regulations or procedures promulgated pursuant thereto."

The House Government Operations Committee objected to the proposal, stating, "The routine use is so broad that, if permissible, it would make all other routine uses unnecessary. If every agency adopted a similar routine use covering all possible disclosures and eliminated all other routine uses, then record subjects would have no idea how federal records might be used. Basic descriptive information about the use of federal records would be hidden behind a veil of bureaucratic generality as was true in the days before passage of the Privacy Act." But CIA Director William J. Casey ignored the objections and the routine use took effect.[7]

How has the government's interpretation of the routine use exemption affected computer matching?

In 1978 when the Department of Health, Education, and Welfare (HEW) wanted to begin its first computer matching project—a comparison of welfare recipient records with federal personnel listings held by the Civil Service Commission (CSC)—government attorneys understood that the Privacy Act was designed precisely to prevent the kind of massive record transfers from one agency to another that the project necessitated. Initially, the CSC's general counsel stated that neither the Privacy Act's routine use exception nor the law enforcement exemption authorized transfer of federal employee rosters to HEW. But the government ignored this advice and invoked the routine use exemption, reasoning that disclosure of federal employment records for an unproven welfare fraud program was compatible with the purpose for which the data were collected. This questionable interpretation was never challenged in court, thus paving the way for a computer matching boom in subsequent years—first under the Carter administration and more so under the Reagan administration.

What is computer matching?

Computer matching is the computerized comparison of two separate record systems that looks to find the same record in both systems—a "raw hit"—usually, for the purpose of finding someone that is defrauding the government. There are as many kinds of computer matches as there are government programs. Files on welfare, food stamp, or Medicaid recipients can be matched against civil service records to see if federal employees are receiving benefits to which they are not entitled. The Supplemental Security Income (SSI) recipients' files are matched against certain IRS records to see if their income matches interest reported by banks with tax returns to verify interest income, and it matches employers' wage reports with tax returns. According to a 1984 estimate by the congressional Office of Technology Assessment (OTA), eleven cabinet level departments and four independent agencies conducted one hundred ten separate matching programs totalling nearly seven hundred matches. Over two billion separate records were used in the reported matching programs, and due to multiple matches of the same records, over seven billion records were matched. Between 1980 and 1984, the number of computer matches had tripled.[8] To date, however, there is not an accurate inventory of computer matching programs.

Do agencies still rely on the Privacy Act's routine use exemption?

Not as much as they used to. Many matches now are mandated by statute. In sum matching has earned Congress's seal of approval. The 1984 Deficit Reduction Act (DEFRA) requires matching for all needs-based social programs.

Doesn't computer matching save a lot of taxpayer dollars?

That's the big question. Undoubtedly, computer matching advocates, led by a community of federal agency inspectors general, say that computer matching has saved millions, maybe billions. In 1985 Department of Health and Human Services (HHS) Inspector General Richard Kusserow wrote that "computer matching and other innovative techniques helped my office identify $1.4 billion in savings—almost a 300 percent increase over the previous year." There are problems with these assertions, however. First, a 1987 HHS report stated that welfare fraud still stood at $1 billion per year, the same figure he gave five years earlier when he recommended widespread computer matching as the primary solution to fraud.[9] Kusserow also admitted that in California's most effective antifraud program, computer matching caught only 12 percent of the fraud cases. About 75 percent of the California fraud and overpayment cases involved problems "that could not be identified or resolved through an automated screen or match," the report said.[10]

In November 1986, after a two-year study of eighteen major computer-matching projects, the GAO declared that the government had not developed a reliable method for evaluating costs and benefits.[11] "Reports of cost-benefit figures [by agencies] did not often detail what cost elements were or were not included or the basis upon which benefit figures were computed," a GAO official testified before Congress. "The information available was not adequate to support a sound decision about whether specific matches were or might be monetarily cost beneficial."[12] Congress had asked GAO to formulate a methodology for evaluating costs and benefits. But GAO admitted being unable to complete the task. "We developed guidelines rather than a formal methodology because of the immaturity of research in this field, because of the diversity of views that exist and because of the informality that still characterizes the varied methods being practiced."[13]

The government consistently has claimed that matching has saved millions of dollars. But after considering the GAO's findings, an impartial observer would be skeptical of the government's claims at best and at worst would sense an outright fraud. Moreover, every time a specific matching project has been scrutinized, the government's savings figures do not hold up.[14]

Why so much discussion about costs and benefits in a book about privacy?

Privacy is seldom an absolute value, but one that is weighed against competing values. In a time of deficits and budgetary restraint, inspectors general created to serve as fraud and abuse watchdogs sold Congress on matching by stating that the threat to privacy was minimal compared to the enormous taxpayer savings that matching would bring.

What privacy issues does matching implicate?

As mentioned before, a key purpose of the Privacy Act was to prevent agency disclosure of personal records, or searches of them, without just cause or individual consent. The laws were intended to assure individuals that their information would not be indiscriminately shuffled between agencies and that data would be collected directly from the individual to the greatest extent practical. As practiced in the US, matching violated these principles and did not appear to save the money its proponents claimed. Matching also implicates traditional privacy values spelled out in the Bill of Rights. A primary purpose of the Fourth Amendment was to preclude random governmental searches by requiring government to show probable cause before conducting a search. However, computer matching entails a random search of records without particularized suspicion toward anyone; the search occurs merely because individuals belong to an identifiable category. It approaches a high-tech form of guilty until proven innocent.

Have people suffered abuse because of government computer-matching programs?

Yes. In fact, the first pilot project, tabbed "Project Match," was an ominous beginning for computer matching. It was developed by Secretary of HEW Joseph Califano, who wanted to show that his department was "getting tough" on welfare cheaters. Washington D.C. area welfare files were matched against US personnel rosters to see if federal employees were accepting benefits illegally. At a November 1977 news conference, Califano announced the names of fifteen "welfare cheaters" which HEW gumshoes "caught" through new matching procedures. Subsequently, however, many of the cases were thrown out for lack of evidence or because the government had failed to stop payments even after recipients reported that they had found jobs. This meant that some women falsely were labeled as cheats. One mother said she received harassing phone calls and her children were taunted at school. Meanwhile, the total "take" of the fifteen welfare mothers was $100,000 (about $6,000 a piece). (The same year, HEW acknowledged spending a greater amount on its twenty-fifth birthday party.) The government recouped no money from the match, but it ended up paying for computer time, investigations, public defenders and other overhead—assuredly more than $100,000.[15]

In 1982 Massachusetts matched public assistance files with private bank records to see if recipients exceeded limits on personal assets. This resulted in the state terminating two thousand recipients without independently verifying the findings or notifying recipients of them. The program exploded in the state's face. Many Social Security numbers, the basis for any match, were incorrect. Initial runs produced over one hundred thousand raw hits, over 90 percent of which reflected government errors. The Massachusetts Law Reform Institute filed a class action suit against the state. Eventually, most of the actions taken because of the match were reversed.[16]

In 1983 the Social Security Administration (SSA) wanted to

match the reported income of Supplemental Security Income (SSI) recipients with IRS files on bank interest. The agency—realizing that it lacked the authority, given strong confidentiality protection for tax records—tried to coerce four million SSI recipients—people who get benefits because they are elderly or severely disabled—into surrendering their privacy rights. SSA notices sent to the recipients warned that if they did not sign a waiver authorizing disclosure of their tax records, their benefits "may be affected." The recipients responded with a class action suit. After years of litigation, the courts ruled that the government violated recipients' privacy rights and ordered it to pay the $25,000 in attorney's fees.[17]

How has Congress responded to these abuses?

In 1984 Congress enacted the Deficit Reduction Act (DEFRA), which authorized computer matching for many social programs but also instituted due process safeguards. These include notifying recipients that their names had been turned up by a match, giving them an opportunity to challenge or explain the findings and barring the termination of benefits solely on the basis of a match.

Has Congress found that additional safeguards were necessary?

Yes. In 1988 Congress passed a law mandating government-wide due process standards for all computer-matching programs. The legislation, the Computer Matching Privacy Protection Act, requires agencies to verify independently all data from matches before taking any adverse actions. Individuals must be given notice and an opportunity to contest any findings. Agencies must sign written agreements before matching and forward them to Congressional committees. Agencies generally will be required to conduct cost-benefit analyses and create "data integrity boards" to oversee privacy and other issues involved in matching projects.

Will this law improve protection for privacy?

By formalizing all aspects of government computer matching, this legislation will curb the worst abuses of privacy that matching has caused. But Congress should also reassess the effectiveness of matching in light of a free-for-all government data-swapping climate. Agency officials often get carried away when they huddle in a room and dream up a new match. For instance, the IRS announced in 1983 that it was experimenting with a pilot project to match marketing firms' profiles of individual incomes against taxpayer records in order to find people who failed to file tax returns. The project was doomed to failure because comparing tax files against marketing estimates is like comparing apples and oranges. The IRS never announced its findings and to date has declined to disclose them under the Freedom of Information Act.

While the computer matching legislation will improve due process and privacy protection, it does not address the more fundamental civil liberties problem of the creation of a "de facto national data file" on each citizen. The trend in government is to increase front-end verification of applicant information for all government benefit programs. Front-end verification has prompted the creation of more centralized data banks against which applicants can be checked. The unchecked growth of verification systems linking various data bases of personal information on every citizen presents a serious danger to individual autonomy and privacy.

Have there been other amendments to the Privacy Act?
Yes. In 1983 Congress approved an amendment to permit disclosure to private credit bureaus of data on people who owe money to the government. Prior to the amendment, such disclosures would have made credit bureaus "government contractors" subject to the access and records management requirements of the Privacy Act, a burden the bureaus did not want to shoulder. The amendment authorized the disclosures while removing the obligation.

What have been the effects of the amendment?
The Reagan administration entered into negotiations to facilitate the disclosure to private credit bureaus of data on people in debt to the government. The result of the new arrangements—reached with Credit Bureau Reports, ACB

Services, and other contractors—has been a significant increase
in the flow of sensitive credit and debt information among
public and private institutions and the establishment of a de
facto national clearinghouse for such records.[18]

Has the US government spied on and harassed its domestic political enemies?

Yes. The best known program was the J. Edgar Hoover
FBI's COINTELPRO of the 1960s and 70s, when the FBI
spied on, infiltrated, and wrote untrue and defamatory letters
and otherwise harassed anti-Vietnam war protestors, the Rev.
Martin Luther King, and other civil rights leaders and political dissidents. The program was exposed through Freedom of
Information Act requests. In subsequent hearings, faced with
the prospect of increased congressional oversight, the post-
Hoover FBI vowed that such political surveillance would no
longer be carried out.

Has that been the case?

Not really. While in recent years the FBI has not cast a
dragnet as wide as that of COINTELPRO, it has more sur-
gically focused on enemies of the Reagan administration's
foreign policy. For instance, the bureau paid an informant
to infiltrate the Dallas office of the Committee in Solidarity
with the People of El Salvador (CISPES), and various FBI
field offices kept tabs on CISPES offices in other cities. The
bureau said it was conducting an "anti-terrorist" probe, but it
continued surveillance long after its own informants and
officials found no reason to believe that CISPES was connected with terrorists. In fact, CISPES members were doing
nothing more than exercising their rights to be politically
active. FBI Director William Sessions eventually admitted
that the CISPES probe was a mistake, but he stopped short of
promising to remove all references to CISPES members from
the bureau's counterintelligence files. CISPES members
responded with a lawsuit seeking to remove and seal all FBI
files on them and generally enforce their rights under the
Privacy Act to ensure that their First Amendment activities
were not recorded by the government.

The FBI also had a program, in conjunction with the US

Customs Service, to interrogate Americans who returned from visits to the Sandinista-run government of Nicaragua.

In Los Angeles, the FBI worked with the Immigration and Naturalization Service to round up seven Palestinians and a Kenyan who distributed literature for the Popular Front for the Liberation of Palestine, even though none of the eight was ever suspected of violence. Represented by ACLU Attorney Paul Hoffman, the "LA 8" challenged the validity of the McCarron-Walter Act, a McCarthy era law which held that aliens are deportable if they advocate world communism or destruction of property or if they belong to a group that does so. On 22 December 1988, US District Judge Stephen V. Wilson of Los Angeles voided as unconstitutional key sections of the McCarron law, as well as a 1987 law allowing the government to ask foreigners if they are members of the PLO when applying for US visas.

In each of these cases, congressional and public pressure apparently forced the FBI to scale down these surveillance programs, proving again in Justice Brandeis's words that "sunshine is the best disinfectant."

Does the government still maintain "hit lists" on its domestic opponents?

Probably, though the number of reported hit lists has declined in recent years. In the early stages of the Reagan administration when conservatives sought to "cleanse" the bureaucracy of "nonloyalists," some agencies compiled hit lists. The US Information Agency in 1984 produced a list of eighty-four liberals who were no longer to be proposed as speakers for agency-sponsored tours abroad. The list included Walter Cronkite, Ralph Nader, Coretta Scott King, Senator Gary Hart, and Representative Jack Brooks. In 1983 the US Interior Department submitted a list of potential advisory committee members to be cleared with the Republican National Committee. And the Environmental Protection Agency drew up a hit list of scientists serving on the EPA's Science Board, describing them as "bleeding heart liberals," "anti-nuclear types," or "snail darter types." Upon exposure in the media, these lists were destroyed, and agencies vowed not to recreate them.[19]

NOTES

1. 5 U.S.C. 552a
2. Sec. Louis Harris opinion survey, The Road After 1984, Tax Impact of Technology, Dec. 7, 1983, funded by Southern New England Telephone Co.
3. *Albright v. U.S.A. (II)*, 732 F.2d. (D.C. Cir. 1984).
4. *Doe v. U.S.A.* 821 F.2d G94 (D.C. Cir. 1987) (en banc).
5. *Privacy Act: Federal Agencies' Implementation Can Be Improved*, GAOGGD-86-107 (Government Printing Office, 1986).
6. *Who Cares About Privacy? Oversight of the Privacy Act of 1974 by the Office of Management and Budget and by the Congress: Eighth Report by the Committee on Government Operations*, Nov. 1, 1983.
7. *Id*.
8. Office of Technology Assessment, *Electronic Record Systems and Individual Privacy* (1986).
9. Office of Inspector General, Department of Health and Human Services, *Report on Welfare Fraud* (1987).
10. *Id*.
11. General Accounting Office, *Computer Matching: Assessing Its Costs and Benefits* (1986).
12. *Hearings on Computer Matching Legislation, House Government Operation Committee, Subcommittee on Government Information, Justice, and Agriculture*, June 23, 1987.
13. *Id*.
14. *See, e.g., Testimony of Norma Rollins*, NYCLU, Sen. Govt. Aff. Comm., Dec. 1982; Washington Post, July 1, 1979, and an unpublished report prepared by Evan Hendricks for Canadian Privacy Commissioner John Grace, 1987.
15. Washington Post, July 1, 1979.
16. *Privacy Times*, Dec. 1, 1982.
17. *Ava P. Traham, et al. v. Donald T. Regan, et al.* No. 82-03004, slip op. (D.C. Cir. July 28, 1987).
18. *Privacy Times*, Nov. 7 and 21, 1984.
19. *Privacy Times*, Feb. 15, 1984, June 8, 1983 and Mar. 16, 1983.

II

Access to Government Records

Can a person gain access to US government records?
Yes. In fact the Freedom of Information Act (FOIA)[1] creates
a stronger right to government records than any other law
does to any other kind of record. Enacted in 1966 and amended
substantially in 1974 and 1986, the FOIA allows everyone in
the world to obtain all records in possession of US executive
branch agencies unless the records fall under one of the nine
exemptions that permit withholding. In addition, the Privacy
Act[2] also allows people access to a more narrow range of
government documents that pertain to themselves. Agencies
that are covered by the FOIA include the Department of
Health and Human Services, the Defense Department, the
Justice Department and its components (such as the Federal
Bureau of Investigation), the Securities and Exchange Commission, and other federal agencies that make up the "alpha-
bet soup" which constitutes the US government. The law also
covers government corporations like Amtrak, the US Postal
Service and the Federal Deposit Insurance Corporation.
While it covers the Office of Management and Budget, it does
not reach the records of the White House staff—whose sole
function is to advise and assist the president—or the records
of Congress. The law does not apply to records of state or local
governments, private business, schools, organizations, or
individuals. Nearly all states and a few cities have their own
open record laws.

Although the term *agency record* is not defined by the
FOIA, it is generally accepted to include documents that are
in possession of and controlled by federal agencies, including
congressionally generated material which ends up in agency
record systems. On the other hand, personal notes and other
semiprivate materials of agency personnel—such as those
maintained in desk drawers—that are not used by a wider
group of agency personnel have been ruled to not constitute
"agency records."

The Privacy Act permits only Americans and permanent
residents to request records on themselves. It defines a *record*

broadly to include any item, collection, or grouping of information about an individual that is maintained by an agency, including his education, financial transactions, medical history, and criminal or employment history and that contains his name, or the identifying number, symbol, or other identifying particular, such as a finger or voice print or a photograph.[3] Under this definition a *record* can be as little as one descriptive item about a person, and it can be part of a larger document, record, or file.

What records are available for access by a requester?
The FOIA requires each agency to make certain information publicly available, even without a specific request. In addition, the FOIA gives a requester access to all agency records upon request, subject to nine exemptions discussed below. The Privacy Act allows a requester access only to his or her personal records maintained by the agency in a system of records.[4] The FOIA begins by requiring each agency to make two categories of records absolutely available (with no exceptions). First, for the guidance of the public, the FOIA requires each agency to publish in the Federal Register:

1. Description of the agency's organization, both in its central office and field offices;
2. Descriptions of the procedures which have been established for obtaining access to agency records, including the places where records are located and the custodian of those records;
3. General descriptions of the agency's functioning and decision-making processes;
4. Agency rules of procedure, description of agency forms along with the places at which such forms may be obtained, and instructions for all the documents, reports, or examinations required by the agency; and
5. Substantive rules of general applicability and statements of general policy formulated and adopted by the agency.[5]

The FOIA directs that a person shall not be bound by any rule, policy statement, or information that is required to be published in the Federal Register but which is not so published, unless that person is given "actual and timely notice of the terms thereof."

The second category of records that must be made available for public inspection and copying are:

1. Final opinions made in the adjudication of particular administrative cases;
2. Statements of policy and interpretations that have been adopted by the agency but not published in the Federal Register;
3. Administrative staff manuals that affect the public; and
4. An index of the information required to be made public.[6]

An agency is authorized to delete personally identifying details contained in any of the above in order to prevent a clearly unwarranted invasion of personal privacy. Such deletions must be explained fully in writing.

In addition, the FOIA provides that "upon any request for records" an agency "shall make the records promptly available to any person" if the requester reasonably describes the desired records clearly and complies with applicable regulations.[7] Therefore, the requester does not have to show any relationship to, or special interest in, the documents requested; the requested documents do not have to be about the person making the request.[8]

The Privacy Act directs that each agency maintaining a system of records shall permit any individual to review or copy any record about that individual which is contained in the system. A system of records means a group of any records from which information is retrieved by the name of the individual or by some identifying number or symbol.[9] Thus, the definition of a system of records focuses on the method of retrieving information from the system: if retrieval is accomplished by reference to a personal identifier (e.g., name, Social Security number), then the system is subject to the Privacy Act. On the other hand, a records system organized by some means other than a personal identifier (e.g., Civil Service grade, date of employment with agency) is not subject to the Privacy Act. The Privacy Protection Study Commission found that some agencies have purposely made their files retrievable by means other than personal identifiers in order to avoid the requirements of the Privacy Act.[10]

But where the FOIA requires agencies to search every record that falls within the scope of a request, the Privacy Act allows certain agencies, particularly those involved in law enforcement, to exempt entire systems of records. In other words, when investigatory, intelligence, and other sensitive documents are sought, an individual can get more records under the FOIA than under the Privacy Act. That's why individuals seeking data on themselves file "joint FOIA/Privacy Act requests."

Can anybody obtain access to agency records?

Yes. The FOIA allows "any person" to request access to agency records.[11] Although not defined in the statute, a person has been interpreted to mean an individual whether or not a citizen of the United States, as well as a business organization, association, or any group of people. The access provisions of the Privacy Act, however, are limited to an individual, defined as a "citizen of the United States or an alien lawfully admitted for permanent residence."[12] This provision was meant to exclude businesses and organizations. The Privacy Act was also meant to exclude CIA and State Department files devoted solely to foreign nationals. The act provides that the parent of a minor or the legal guardian of an individual who has been declared to be incompetent may act on behalf of that individual.[13]

Can a person obtain access to documents without the help of a lawyer?

Yes. Both the FOIA and Privacy Act establish simple procedures for obtaining access to agency documents. It is not necessary to have a lawyer make a request for documents or to follow that request through the administrative process. Of course, if the requester later decides to bring a lawsuit challenging an agency decision, the assistance of a lawyer may be necessary.

How can a person obtain access to agency records?

A request for records can be in the form of a simple letter[14] to the head of the agency that controls or maintains the records. The first step in requesting records is to identify the agency maintaining or controlling the desired records. In most instances this will not be difficult. People looking for personal records usually make a request to agencies with which they have had contact, such as agencies which have employed, served, or investigated the individual. A person who is not certain which agency has the desired records can write to the agencies likely to maintain relevant records. It may help to consult the Government Organizational Manual, which identifies and describes the functions of all federal agencies. The manual is available in most libraries and may be purchased from the Government Printing Office in Washington D.C.

A letter to the agency requesting access to personal records should begin by stating that the request is being made pursuant to the FOIA and the Privacy Act.[15] To speed processing, both the envelope and the letter should be clearly marked "FOIA/PA Request."

The FOIA requires that the requester "reasonably describe" the records requested. The agency must advise you if it considers your request too vague to process. Generally, agency personnel will assist you in reformulating your request to conform to the applicable standards of specificity. If a person wants only his or her documents, it is usually sufficient to ask for "all records about me." Under the Privacy Act there is usually not much difficulty describing the requested records because, as defined by the act, records are limited to personally identifiable information contained in a records system.

For large agencies divided into many smaller units, the request should identify the particular departments having files. For example, if writing to the Justice Department, the requester should indicate if the request is for records maintained by the Criminal Division, Immigration and Naturalization Service, or other division within the agency. It is permissible to ask for a search of the files of more than one department, but the requester may, instead, write separately to each department. Generally, a person seeking access to agency documents located in offices in different places should address a separate request to each location. For example, a person requesting FBI documents located in files both at headquarters in Washington D.C. and in the Albany, New York, office should address a separate request to each office. Similarly, the Department of Health and Human Services is a huge agency with components like the Social Security Administration, the Food and Drug Administration, and the Health Care Financing Administration. If you are certain that one of those divisions has the records you want, then you can address your request directly to their FOIA/PA offices. The same goes for the Defense Department, which includes the Army, Navy, Air Force, and Marines and divisions like the Defense Intelligence Agency and the Defense Security Assistance Agency. In fact, even military bases have their own FOIA offices.

The letter to the agency should also include your full name and address. Many agencies require that your signature be notarized when seeking data on yourself. All of this information is required so that the agency does not release personal information to people using false identification.

Finally, each agency is authorized to promulgate regulations governing the procedures for making FOIA and Privacy Act requests to that agency.[16] These regulations are available in the Federal Register. In addition, you may write to the agency itself for its regulations or simply ask for a copy of them in your request letter. If your request letter does not conform to the agency's regulations, the agency will respond by describing its defects and explaining how they may be corrected. In most instances, the agency personnel can be contacted directly for help in resolving any difficulties.

Does the government have to permit access to all requested agency records?

No. The FOIA contains nine exemptions which permit the agency to withhold information.[17] The Privacy Act also exempts certain agencies and categories of documents from its access provisions.[18]

THE FOIA EXEMPTIONS

Exemption 1 allows the government to withhold data that have been classified properly according to executive order—

in this case Executive Order 12356, issued by President Reagan in 1982. The Reagan order expanded governmental secrecy powers by removing a previous requirement, established by President Carter, that withholding was only justified when disclosure "could reasonably be expected to cause identifiable damage" to the national defense or foreign relations of the United States. In addition to removing the "damage" standard, the Reagan order for the first time allowed agencies to reclassify data that already had been declassified.

A broad range of data can be kept secret under Exemption 1, including military plans, weapons, or operations, foreign government information and files relating to foreign relations, certain scientific and technology data related to the national security, material on nuclear facilities, and any other intelligence and defense records classified "top secret," "secret" or "confidential" under the Reagan order.

In 1985 Congress approved a special law exempting the Central Intelligence Agency's operational files from the search requirements of the FOIA. The reasoning was that data in CIA operational files were exempt anyway under Exemption 1, and that relieving the CIA of the burden of searching through these files would free its personnel to provide faster service to requesters seeking data located in other CIA record systems.

Exemption 2 exempts matters that are related solely to the internal personnel rules and practices of an agency. For the most part, this exemption applies only to minor matters not of significant public interest. The Supreme Court has recognized that Exemption 2 may be invoked to withhold matters of some public interest where necessary to prevent circumvention of agency regulations. For example, an agency may withhold investigative manuals used by the agency in its regulatory function.

Exemption 3 authorizes the withholding of matters specifically protected by another statute, but only if that other statute mandates withholding, establishes particular criteria, and refers to particular types of information. Congress has passed a number of statutes which satisfy these requirements. For example, separate laws specify that personal tax data, the internal structure of the CIA, charges of employment discrimination, and individually identifiable census data are guaranteed confidentiality and therefore may be withheld under FOIA Exemption 3.[19] Statutes that merely permit the discretionary withholding of information are not specific enough to satisfy the strict requirements of this exemption.

Exemption 4 exempts trade secrets and privileged or confidential commercial or financial information. A trade secret is generally defined as a "formula, patent device or compilation of information which is used in one's business and which gives [that person] an advantage over competitors who do not know it or use it."[20] A large body of law that has developed independent of the FOIA governs the application of this exemption. These matters usually arise only in commercial, rather than personal, FOIA cases. The second category of exempt information is confidential or privileged commercial or financial information obtained from a person. Commercial or financial information is considered to be confidential if disclosure of the information is likely either: (1) to impair the government's ability to obtain necessary information in the future; or (2) to cause substantial harm to the competitive position of the person from whom the information was obtained."[21] The requirement that the information be obtained from "a person" precludes the application of this exemption to information generated by the government.

Exemption 5 applies to information that would be privileged in civil litigation such as matters covered by the attorney-client privilege, the work-product privilege, and executive privilege. The attorney-client privilege covers confidential communications between attorney and client, and the work-product privilege covers material prepared for trial or in anticipation of litigation. Both privileges have received extensive comment and court consideration independent of the FOIA, and the application of this exemption requires reference to that body of law. The government alone can invoke an executive privilege for "materials reflecting deliberative or policy making processes" as opposed to "purely factual investigative matters."[22] The executive privilege is intended to insulate the deliberative process from public disclosure, thus encouraging uninhibited policy discussions. It generally applies only to predecisional records.

Exemption 6 authorizes the agency to withhold personnel and medical files and "similar files the disclosure of which would constitute a clearly unwarranted invasion of personal privacy." The Supreme Court has said that the implementation of this exemption requires a balancing of the individual's expectation of privacy against the public benefits derived from opening agency action to public scrutiny. The statute's protection for only "clearly unwarranted" invasions of privacy has been interpreted to mean that the balance should be tilted in favor of disclosure.

Exemption 7 covers investigatory records compiled for law enforcement purposes, but only to the extent that production of such law enforcement records or information

1. could reasonably be expected to interfere with enforcement proceedings,
2. would deprive a person of a right to a fair trial or an impartial adjudication,
3. could reasonably be expected to constitute an unwarranted invasion of personal privacy,
4. could reasonably be expected to disclose the identity of a confidential source, including a state, local or foreign agency or authority or any private institution which furnished information on a confidential basis, and, in the case of a record of information compiled by a criminal law enforcement authority in the course of a criminal investigation, information furnished by a confidential source,
5. would disclose techniques and procedures for law enforcement investigations or prosecutions, or would disclose guidelines for law enforcement investigations or prosecutions if such disclosure could reasonably be expected to risk circumvention of the law, or
6. could reasonably be expected to endanger the life or physical safety of any individual.

The 1986 Amendments to the FOIA also permit law enforcement agencies to "refuse to confirm or deny" the existence of records that involve an ongoing investigation or trial and disclosure might interfere with them or when the records pertain to an informant's identity or to counterintelligence.

Exemption 8 protects records related to the examination, operation or condition of certain financial institutions subject to federal regulation. And exemption 9 exempts geological and geophysical information and data.

Although the FOIA authorizes an agency to withhold information falling within the nine exempt categories, the statute does not require withholding; the government can release information even if it falls within the exemptions. Therefore, an individual desiring access to information should make the request even if it may appear to be exempt.

Is there any way to appeal an agency decision to withhold information?

Yes. The FOIA provides that if an agency denies any document, in whole or in part, the individual has a right to an administrative appeal.[23] Under the FOIA, a letter telling the requester that all or part of the request has been denied must also tell of the right to appeal and say where the appeal should be directed. The person deciding the appeal must be the head of the agency or his designee and must be superior to the employee responsible for the original denial.

A letter of appeal[24] should state clearly that it is made under the FOIA, state briefly what records are requested, and describe the original agency decision, including the dates of relevant correspondence. It may help to include a copy of the original request letter and the agency letter denying that request.

An appeal letter does not have to include arguments in support of the request for documents. It is sufficient merely to state that the original agency decision is appealed. The FOIA puts the burden on the government to sustain the decision not to release the records. Very often it is impossible to prepare a rebuttal on appeal because the agency gives the requester so little explanation of its rationale. However, if the requester knows why the agency is refusing to release the records and can identify specific arguments refuting the agency's contentions, it is worthwhile to include those arguments in the appeal letter.

Unlike the FOIA, the Privacy Act does not provide a right to administrative appeal. Many agencies nonetheless offer an appeal procedure employing the same mechanisms established for FOIA matters. If it denies the request, the agency will inform the requester of applicable procedures.

If the appeal process is available, it should be used in all cases in which the agency has not fully satisfied the request for documents. There are several reasons to appeal. First, the appeal may result in the release of additional records. Even though the appeal is within the same agency, it is decided by people other than those making the original decision; the appellate authority is often more distant from the records and has less of a proprietary interest in protecting them from release. Second, the appeal is a simple process which does not require investment of much time or resources. Third, the appeal is an absolute prerequisite for bringing a court action to challenge the agency denial of an FOIA request. If the appeal does not result in the release of all the requested records, the requester is entitled to challenge the agency denial in court.

Is the government required to respond promptly to requests for documents?

Yes. The FOIA provides that any agency must decide within ten working days after receipt of a request whether to comply. It must then immediately notify the requester of the decision and the reasons.[25] If the requested records are denied, in whole or in part, the agency must advise the requester of the right to an appeal. If the requester appeals, the appeal must be decided within twenty working days after receipt by an agency.[26] If the decision is adverse the agency must advise of the right to judicial review.

In "unusual circumstances" the FOIA allows an agency to extend, for no more than ten working days, the period allowed for the initial determination and the period allowed for the appeal determination.[27] The act limits unusual circumstances to cases where the agency must (1) search for requested documents in field facilities or other offices, (2) search for and examine voluminous separate records demanded in a single request, or (3) consult with another agency having a substantial interest in the determination. If the agency invokes this provision, it must write to the requester, stating why the extension is needed and when the final determination is expected.

Unlike the FOIA, the Privacy Act does not require prompt response to a request for documents. However, implementing regulations prepared by the Office of Management and Budget (OMB) establishes standards. Agencies should acknowledge requests within ten working days; whenever practicable, the agency should also decide whether access can be granted within those first ten working days but in any event should decide and notify the requester in writing within thirty working days. If access is granted, the requester should receive the records within thirty working days; if, for good cause, the agency is unable to do so (for example, if the record is inactive and stored in a records center), it should inform the requester in writing that there will be a delay and of how long it is expected to be.[28]

Despite explicit time limits established by the FOIA and more lenient limits imposed by Privacy Act regulations, agencies rarely comply. Many agencies are deluged with requests and do not have the capacity for timely response. (Recently, the FBI was taking more than a year to respond to FOIA requests.) Except in emergencies, the requester has few alternatives but to wait.

Can an agency be compelled to speed up the processing of an FOIA request?

In most instances, no. When an agency delays, the FOIA allows the requester to challenge the agency in court, but in most cases the court will stay proceedings pending completion of agency processing.

The FOIA provides that an agency's failure to respond within the statutory time period is a denial of the request.[29] Therefore if an agency fails to respond within ten working days (or twenty days with an extension), the requester can proceed to the next step—appeal. If the agency fails to respond to the appeal within twenty days (or thirty days with an extension), then the requester can consider that delay a final denial and file a complaint in court challenging the agency's failure to release the records.

The act also provides that if such an action is begun, the court may stay the case to allow the agency to finish the administrative processing if "exceptional circumstances exist and the agency is exercising due diligence in responding to the request. . . ."[30] In at least one jurisdiction, courts have decided that the mere fact of an agency backlog of FOIA requests is sufficient to satisfy the "exceptional circumstances" test.[31] Even where the government must show exceptional circumstances and due diligence, courts have not usually required the government to comply with the time requirements of the FOIA, except in emergencies. If the requester has a special and urgent need for the records, the court may require the agency to process the records expeditiously. For example, if an individual is about to begin a criminal trial and the FOIA request is for documents necessary for the defense, the court may require the agency to accelerate the processing.[32] But most requests, particularly complex or controversial ones, will take months and even years. If the request leads to a lawsuit the duration can be two to ten years. A key to successful use of the FOIA is persistence.

Do requesters have to pay agencies for providing documents?

Most of the time, yes. The FOIA authorizes agencies to charge both search and duplicating fees. The Privacy Act authorizes only duplicating fees. Of course, the amount charged depends on the difficulty in locating the documents and the volume of records to be disclosed. As of 1988 most agencies charge a standard search fee of fifteen dollars per hour; copying charges range from ten to twenty-five cents per page. Agencies can require requesters to put down a "deposit" if the estimated cost will exceed $250 or if the requester previously failed to pay fees. FOIA fees range from twenty-five to thousands of dollars.

Do requesters always have to pay?

No. The government must waive or at least reduce fees when "disclosure of the information is in the public interest because it is likely to contribute significantly to public understanding of the operations or activities of the government and is not primarily in the commercial interest of the requester." It also must only charge for duplication costs when "records are not sought for commercial use and the request is made by an educational or noncommercial scientific institution, whose purpose is scholarly or scientific research; or a representative of the news media."

Fees have always been controversial. Regular users of the

FOIA accused some agencies of imposing high fees to impede access to documents even though the law required reduction or waiver of fees when disclosure was in the public interest.

Congressional supporters of the more specific standard, adopted as part of the 1986 FOIA Amendments, said it was intended to encourage the government to grant fee waivers generously. However after two years under the standard, most agencies—with the Justice Department taking the lead—have continued to be miserly with FOIA requesters.[33]

What can requesters do if an agency denies them access to documents or fee waivers?

The requester can sue the agency in federal court. Upon completion of all administrative appeals, the FOIA and Privacy Act provide that action may be filed in a federal court (1) where the requester lives or (2) has a principal place of business, (3) where the records are located or (4) in Washington D.C.

The two laws require courts to review independently all agency decisions to withhold records. Courts can order agencies to disclose entire records or portions of them. They also can order agencies to live up to their obligation to provide requesters with a comprehensive index of withheld records, a valuable resource in itself. In special cases, courts have exercised their power to inspect withheld records to see if they, or parts of them, should be disclosed. Courts also can discipline federal officials who flout the law's disclosure requirements. Since 1974, when the FOIA was strengthened by post-Watergate amendments, hundreds of lawsuits have succeeded at forcing the government to release thousands of previously secret documents.

Do you have to have a lawyer to file a lawsuit?

No. There are many instances of nonlawyers taking their own FOIA requests to court. In fact the American Civil Liberties Union annually publishes a litigation manual edited by Allan Adler, an attorney and leading FOIA expert, which provides step-by-step instructions on filing a lawsuit. Of course, if you can afford one, it's preferable to have an attorney who specializes in the FOIA represent you to maximize your chances of success.

Does the government ever have to pay your attorney's fees and costs?

Yes. The FOIA and the Privacy Act authorize the court to assess reasonable attorney's fees and costs against the United States if the plaintiff has "substantially prevailed." In reaching its determination, the court must consider (1) the benefit to the public, if any, deriving from the case, (2) the commercial benefit of the requester, (3) the nature of the requester's interest in the records sought, and (4) whether the government's withholding of the records sought had a reasonable basis in law. Attorneys representing FOIA requesters have been awarded hundreds of thousands of dollars in fees because courts felt in these cases agencies unreasonably withheld records and the public benefitted from the forced disclosure of records.

What kinds of information have been disclosed because of FOIA requests?

Since FOIA applies to all agencies of the government, it has prompted release of an enormous variety of data. It was the FOIA which helped uncover government-held documents about the Ford Pinto's exploding gas tank and about the unsafe Firestone 500 tires. Nuclear safety problems and new data on toxic waste dumps were also made known because of the FOIA. The law helped journalists expose FBI's COINTELPRO, a massive, illegal program of spying on and harassing political activists during the late 1960s and early 1970s. And FOIA requesters have helped shed new light on important foreign policy matters such as the Cuban missile crisis, CIA coups in the Third World, and the Iran rescue mission.

Furthermore, the act has proven to be a gold mine for historians; they have been able to reach thousands of pages of material concerning America's past.[34]

What has been the government's attitude toward the FOIA?

First, the good news. Agencies have FOIA offices responsible for handling requests. These offices usually are run by officials who have worked with the law for years. Known as "access professionals," these officials respect the FOIA's goals and are committed to furnishing to FOIA requesters as many documents as efficiently as possible, given the sometimes huge volume of requests and the severely cut back staff. It is from these offices that, voluntarily or by court order, millions of government documents and former secrets have been disclosed to the public.

What's the bad news?

Despite the FOIA, secrecy remains the natural law of government. Moreover, the Reagan administration fought especially hard against the public's access to information in general and the FOIA in particular. It cut back on publications, curtailed access to reading rooms, and reduced library budgets. It sought amendments that would have reduced severely the kinds of information available under the FOIA. When that effort failed it issued executive orders encouraging government secrecy. It advised agencies to be miserly with FOIA fee waivers, despite congressional direction to the contrary, and it told agencies that the Justice Department would be ready to defend nearly any agency decision to keep secrets. It promoted secrecy agreements for officials who might see "classifiable data" and polygraph tests of those who might leak confidential data.

Has computerization of government records affected the public's right under the FOIA?

While it's still early to give a definitive answer, an authoritative congressional study has concluded that the advent of electronic storage and dissemination has created "gray areas" in the law and led to inconsistent access policies among federal agencies. The report, authored by the Office of Technology Assessment (OTA), recommended amendments to the FOIA that would affirm the public's right to electronic data held by the government. The October 1988 report stated:

> For the 1990s and beyond, Congress needs to decide whether the FOIA should continue to be viewed as an 'access to records' statute or whether it should be perceived more broadly as an 'access to information' statute, . . . Due to the explosive growth in electronic information storage, processing and transmission by the federal government, traditional views about records and

searches need to be modified to ensure even basic access to public information. . .[35]

If the statutory language is not modified to address electronic information, agencies may have new opportunities to legally withhold certain classes of materials from the public. The case law in many areas is too limited, conflicting or vague to give comprehensive or consistent direction to agencies and courts. Variation in agency practice calls for stronger legislative guidance. If Congress wishes to maintain the integrity of the FOIA in an electronic environment, the goals of the statute should be reassessed, and statutory amendment pursued.[36]

Have there been precedents on public access to the government's electronic data?

Only a few. In one case, *Yeager v. DEA*, a US Court of Appeals ruled that an agency did not have to use its computers to manipulate data so otherwise exempt data could be disclosed.[37] However, in that case, as well as *Long v. IRS*, courts have ruled that using a computer's capabilities to delete exempt material from computerized records did not constitute the creation of a new record and therefore did not justify denying access to nonexempt information.[38]

As of 1988, probably the most important decision was made by the Energy Department's Office of Hearings and Appeals, which reversed a Department of Energy (DOE) component's decision to deny a private library access to computer-stored nuclear information. The appeals office said that to the extent the DOE component had records in a database and software capable of searching it, the DOE component was required by the FOIA to search the database for the requested records.

George B. Breznay, director of DOE's Office of Hearings and Appeals, said "[a] search of this nature is not, in substance, significantly different from a search of a file cabinet for paper records that are responsive to a request. If the FOIA required anything less it would allow agencies to conceal information from public scrutiny by placing it in computerized form. This would be inconsistent with the FOIA policy of the fullest possible disclosure."

Are any government databases designed to facilitate public access?

Yes. The most notable example is the Environmental Protection Agency's Toxic Release Inventory (TRI), which facilitates the public's right to know about hazardous chemicals. Created by the 1986 Superfund Amendments, the TRI database is filled with data collected by the EPA, but which can be extracted according to the wishes of each database user. This was the first statute requiring a federal agency to collect significant public data and then distribute them by electronic means. Hopefully, the standards will be applied to future government database projects.

Are there provisions for penalizing a federal official who improperly withholds requested records?

Yes, but the FOIA penalty provision is extremely limited, and the Privacy Act does not contain a penalty provision. The FOIA provides that when a court orders the production of improperly withheld agency records and assesses attorney's fees and costs against the United States and, in addition, the court issues a written finding that the circumstances raise questions whether agency personnel acted arbitrarily or capriciously, the Office of Personnel Management (OPM) shall promptly initiate a proceeding to determine if disciplinary action is warranted.[39] The commission shall investigate and submit its findings and recommendations to the administrative authority with responsibility for the agency, which shall take the corrective action recommended by the commission. The penalty provision applies to all employees of agencies subject to the FOIA.

However, the FOIA penalty provision has rarely been invoked, and there is no reason to believe that the threat of sanctions acts as a deterrent to arbitrary or capricious agency withholdings.

Can a person obtain access to state and local government records?

Perhaps, depending on state and local laws and regulations. The federal FOIA does not apply to state and local government records, but most states have laws or regulations providing some access to government records. Many of the state statutes are patterned on the federal FOIA. There are many variations from state to state, and it is beyond the scope of this book to detail them all.

A person desiring access to state and local government records may:

1. Seek the advice of a lawyer familiar with the state or local freedom-of-information law (many local bar associations will help people to contact a lawyer with the requisite skills).
2. Read the law—applicable state statutes can be found in all law libraries; many public libraries maintain a set of the state statutes.
3. Write to the state agency maintaining the requested records and simply request access. In most cases the agency will advise the requester if the request has failed to satisfy the procedures of the state law or if the requested records are exempt under state law. Of course, this process may result in delay but, for the requester who does not have access to information about the state statute, it may be the easiest first step.

NOTES

1. 5 U.S.C. § 552.
2. 5 U.S.C. § 552a.
3. 5 U.S.C. § 552a (a) (4).
4. 5 U.S.C. § 552a (a) (5).
5. 5 U.S.C. § 552 (a) (1).
6. 5 U.S.C. § 552 (a) (2).
7. 5 U.S.C. § 552 (a) (3).
8. However, although a person cannot be denied access to documents merely because those documents are about another person, the information about another person may be deleted by the agency pursuant to exemptions protecting personal privacy. See exemptions 6 and 7 (c), § 5 U.S.C. 552 (b) (6) and (b) 7 (c) and text accompanying footnote 22.
9. 5 U.S.C. § 552a (a) (5).
10. Privacy Protection Study Commission, *Personal Privacy in an Informational Society*, 504 (1977).
11. 5 U.S.C. § 552 (a) (3).

12. 5 U.S.C. § 552a (a) (2).
13. 5 U.S.C. § 552a (h).
14. A sample request letter is included as Appendix A.
15. 5 U.S.C. § 552 (a) (3); 5 U.S.C. § 552a (d).
16. 5 U.S.C. § 552 (a) (4) (A); 5 U.S.C. § 552a (e) (4).
17. 5 U.S.C. § 552 (b).
18. 5 U.S.C. § 552 (j) and (k).
19. 26 U.S. § 6103 of the U.S. tax code. 50 U.S.C. § 403g, 42 U.S.C. § 2000 (e), 13 U.S.C. § 9 respectively.
20. Restatement of Torts, 757, comment (b) (1939).
21. *National Parks and Conservation Ass'n v. Morton*, 498 F. 2d 765, 770 (D.C. Cir. 1974).
22. *EPA v. Mink*, 410 U.S. 73, 89 (1973). *See generally* Dorsen and Shattuck, *Executive Privilege, the Congress and the Courts*, 35 Ohio St. L.J. 1 (1974).
23. 5 U.S.C. § 552 (a) (6) (A).
24. A sample letter of appeal is included as Appendix B.
25. 5 U.S.C. § 552 (a) (6) (A) (i).
26. 5 U.S.C. § 552 (a) (6) (A) (ii).
27. 5 U.S.C. § 552 (a) (6) (B).
28. Office of Management and Budget, *Privacy Act Guidelines*, (d) (i) 40 Fed. Reg. 28, 949, 28, 958 (1975).
29. 5 U.S.C. § 552 (a) (7) (C).
30. 5 U.S.C. § 552 (a) (6) (C).
31. *Open America v. Watergate Special Prosecution Force*, 547 F. 2d 605 (D.C. Cir. 1975).
32. *Cleaver v. Kelley*, 427 F. Supp. 80 (D.C. 1976).
33. See Hearings of the Senate Judiciary Committee *Subcommittee on Law and Technology*, 100th Congress, Second Session, Aug. 2, 1988.
34. Evan Hendricks, *Former Secrets*, Campaign For Political Rights (1982).
35. Office of Technology Assessment, *Informing the Nation: Federal Information Dissemination in an Electronic Age* (1988).
36. *Id*.
37. *Yeager v. DEA*, 678 F. 2d 315 (D.C. Cir. 1982).
38. *Long v. IRS*, 596 F. 2d 362 (9th Cir. 1979).
39. 5 U.S.C. § 552 (a) (4) (F).

III

Correction of Government Records

Is there any way for a person to correct or amend agency records?

Yes. The Privacy Act requires that each agency maintaining a system of records shall permit a person to request amendment of a record pertaining to that individual.[1] (The Freedom of Information Act, however, contains only access provisions and does not afford an individual any right to correct or amend the information in the file.) This provision applies to all federal executive agencies, independent regulatory agencies, and private contractors that operate systems of records for any agency to accomplish this function.[2] It pertains only to records about the individual seeking the amendment and only if such a record is maintained in an agency system of records. A system of records means any group of records from which information is retrieved by reference to the name or other identifying symbol of the individual.[3] An individual, under the terms of the Privacy Act, must be a United States citizen or a permanent resident alien.[4]

On what grounds may a person seek correction or amendment of agency records?

The Privacy Act requires that agencies maintain records that are accurate, relevant, timely, and complete.[5] A person may request amendment of any record which fails to satisfy one or more of those standards.[6] The act does not define the terms, but it provides some clues. In describing the record-keeping requirements imposed on the federal agencies, the Privacy Act says they shall "maintain all records which are used by the agency in making any determination about any individual with such accuracy, relevance, timeliness and completeness, as is reasonably necessary to assure fairness to the individual in the determination."[7] The meaning of relevance is somewhat further described by the requirement that each agency "maintain in its records only such information about an individual as is relevant and necessary to accomplish a purpose of the agency. . . ."[8] The 'relevance" and the "completeness" standards, in conjunction, require that agencies eliminate all extraneous information and, at the same time, include in the records all of the information necessary for their proper use. "Accuracy" and "timeliness" are not defined. In some instances the issue will be the truth or falsity of an objective fact, such as the date of an event, the status of an employment relationship, or the disposition of an arrest. In other cases, accuracy will involve more subjective judgments and will be more difficult to demonstrate. For example, the reason a person left a previous job may be perceived differently by the employee and the employer. Questions of "timeliness" involve similar subjective judgments. As with relevance, it seems appropriate to look to whether dated information is necessary to accomplish a purpose of the agency. Until these matters are settled in the courts, there are no generally applicable criteria to determine when a bit of information becomes too stale.

The provisions for amending records do not permit the alteration of evidence that has been presented in judicial or administrative proceedings. Any changes to such evidentiary records must be made according to the rules governing those proceedings. Similarly, the Privacy Act does not permit the individual to challenge information which has already been the subject of judicial or administrative action. For example, a person can not use the Privacy Act to challenge the accuracy of a conviction record on the grounds that the conviction was improper. However, a person could seek amendment of a record which improperly described the details of the conviction.

How does a person challenge the accuracy, relevancy, timeliness, or completeness of agency records?

The procedures for amending or expunging records are similar to the procedures for gaining access to records. The individual must write to the agency; the agency will then process the request administratively; and the individual can obtain court review if the request is denied.

First, of course, a requester must obtain access to the agency records to see what they say.[9] When the agency sends those records, it should describe the procedures for challenging the records.

The Privacy Act requires each agency to establish procedures for reviewing a request from an individual concerning the amendment of a record, making a determination on that request for amendment, and providing for an appeal within the agency if there is an adverse determination.[10] The applicable procedures may be obtained from the agency itself or may be found in the Federal Register. Although the specific details may vary from agency to agency, the procedures are generally similar. The request for amendment should be made in writing, even though some agencies may permit an oral request in person or on the telephone. A written request will be important later in the amendment process if the request is denied. If a written request is inadequate in some respect, or fails to satisfy the agency prerequisites, the agency should advise the requester of the defects and how they can be corrected. To verify an individual's identity the agency may require an address, Social Security number, and notarized signature. It may save some time to include that information in the original request for amendment. The letter to the agency should describe briefly the objectionable information, the grounds of the objection (the reason for believing the record is inaccurate, irrelevant, outdated, or incomplete), and the changes requested.

The Privacy Act requires that an amendment request must be acknowledged within ten working days and "promptly" decided.[11] Applicable regulations provide that the request for correction should also be decided, wherever practicable, within ten business days, so that the acknowledgment and the decision will be contained in one letter. In any event the amendment request should be completed "as soon as reasonably possible," normally within thirty working days from the receipt of the request.[12] If the agency refuses to amend the record, it must inform the individual of the reasons and instruct him how to seek a review of that refusal by the head of the agency.[13]

Does a person have recourse if a request for amendment is denied?

Yes. If a request for amendment is denied, the agency must give the individual the right to appeal to the head of the agency or his designee. In addition, the Privacy Act allows a person denied an amendment to insert a concise statement of disagreement in the record.

Unlike the access provisions of the Privacy Act, the amendment provisions of the act require that when an agency refuses to make a requested change the individual must be given the right to appeal.[14] In its letter denying the amendment request, the agency must describe the procedures for appeal and the name of the individual to whom that appeal should be directed. The appeal letter should describe the original request and the initial agency denial (it may help to enclose copies of the earlier correspondence) and ask that the original agency denial be reviewed. If the individual has additional reasons for making the amendment, those reasons should be briefly stated.

The Privacy Act requires that the agency must decide the appeal within thirty business days from the date the review is requested. The head of the agency may extend that deadline by an additional thirty days if there is "good cause shown."[15] If the appeal is denied, the appeals officer must state, in writing, the reasons and must advise the requester of the right to file a statement of disagreement and the right to judicial review. If the requester does file a statement of disagreement, the agency may also include in the record a concise statement of its reasons for not making the requested amendments. The requester's statement of disagreement must be provided to anyone to whom the disputed information is subsequently disclosed.

Can a person bring a lawsuit to compel the agency to make the requested amendment?

Yes. The Privacy Act provides that whenever an agency makes a determination not to amend an individual's record, the United States district courts shall have jurisdiction to determine the controversy.[16] The court may order the agency to amend the record in accordance with the request or in another way.

Before bringing a lawsuit, however, the individual must exhaust all administrative remedies—that is, the initial request and appeal must have been denied. As with an access lawsuit, a lawsuit to correct may be filed in the district where the individual resides or has a principal place of business, where the agency records are kept, or in the District of Columbia.[17] Furthermore, an individual must bring a lawsuit within two years after the cause of action arises (when the agency finally denies the request for amendment) or, if an agency has misrepresented information that is material to establishing the agency's liability, within two years after discovery of the misrepresentation.[18]

In an amendment lawsuit, the Privacy Act does not specify whether the individual has the principal burden of convincing the court that the agency's decision was wrong or whether the government must bear the burden of establishing that its decision was correct. This issue — which partly has the burden of proof — is yet to be resolved by the courts. The regulations of the OMB note that the burden was not expressly placed on the agency and concludes that the omission was "intended to result in placing the burden of challenging the accuracy of the record upon the individual."[19]

The Privacy Act clearly provides that the court may assess costs and attorney's fees against the United States if the requester "substantially prevails."[20] The attorney's fees and costs provision of the Privacy Act are identical to the corresponding provisions of the FOIA and are likely to be subject to similar interpretations.[21]

Are any agency records exempt from the Privacy Act amendment provisions?

Yes. The agency records that are excluded from operation of the Privacy Act access provisions are also excluded from the amendment provisions.[22] Although the amendment provisions of the Privacy Act do not apply to records maintained by many important agencies (such as the CIA, the Secret Service, and — in most instances — the FBI), records of most social service and personnel agencies (e.g. HHS and OPM commission) are subject to the amendment provisions.

Does an agency have to correct inaccuracies in records that were disseminated before the record was amended?

Yes. If an agency amends a record in compliance with a request or order, it must notify prior recipients of that record of the changes. If the prior recipients are other federal agencies, they must also correct their records.[23] Similarly, if the record is not amended, and the individual files a statement of disagreement, that statement must be sent to prior recipients of the record.[24]

The agency's duty to notify prior recipients is tied to its obligation, under the Privacy Act, to keep an accounting of its disclosures of personal records to other agencies or individuals.[25] This requirement excludes disclosures to employees of the agency having a need to know the information or disclosures made pursuant to the Freedom of Information Act. However, the obligation to maintain such an accounting was first imposed only when the Privacy Act became effective on 27 September 1975. Therefore, even if a record is amended or a statement of disagreement is filed, the agency will not be able to identify agencies or individuals that may have received the records before then.

NOTES

1. 5 U.S.C. § 552a (d) (2).
2. 5 U.S.C. § 552a (a) (1) and (m).
3. 5 U.S.C. § 552a (a) (5).
4. 5 U.S.C. § 552a (a) (2).
5. 5 U.S.C. § 552a (e) (5).
6. 5 U.S.C. § 552a (d) (2).
7. 5 U.S.C. § 552a (e) (5).
8. 5 U.S.C. § 552a (e) (1).
9. The procedures for obtaining access to documents are explained in chapter 14.
10. 5 U.S.C. § 552a (f) (4).
11. 5 U.S.C. § 552a (d) (2) (B).
12. Office of Management and Budget, Privacy Act Guidelines (d) (2) (A), 40 Fed. Reg. 28,949, 28,958 (1975).
13. 5 U.S.C. § 552a (d) (2) (B) (ii).
14. 5 U.S.C. § 552a (d) (3).
15. *Id*.
16. 5 U.S.C. § 552a (g) (2).
17. 5 U.S.C. § 552a (g) (5).
18. 5 U.S.C. § 552a (g) (5).
19. 5 U.S.C. § 552a (g) (5).
20. 5 U.S.C. § 552a (g) (3) (B).
21. 5 U.S.C. § 552 (a) (4) (E).

22. 5 U.S.C. § 552a (j) and (k);
23. 5 U.S.C. § 552a (c) (4).
24. *Id*.
25. 5 U.S.C. § 552a (c).

IV

Criminal Justice Records

Which agencies keep arrest and conviction records?

All of the agencies that constitute the criminal justice system keep records of arrests and convictions: police, prosecutors, courts, probation departments, prisons, parole boards, and the many subsidiary agencies that serve each of these.

The Federal Bureau of Investigation maintains records with arrest and conviction information submitted by local, state, and federal agencies. A federal statute authorizes the FBI, as the agent of the attorney general, to "acquire, collect, classify, and preserve identification, criminal identification, crime, and other records" and to "exchange these records with, and for the official use of, authorized officials of the federal government, the states, cities, and penal and other institutions."[1]

How many people in the United States have an arrest record?

Between one-fourth and one-third of the total work force has a criminal history record, according to a 1985 survey.[2] It is likely that minorities are the subject of a disproportionately high number of criminal records since blacks are arrested four times more frequently than whites. Nearly half of those arrests of blacks did not end in conviction. In 1980, blacks accounted for about 29 percent of all records in the FBI's files, nearly triple the percentage of blacks in this country.[3]

The FBI maintains data about individuals who have been arrested on a document known as an identification record, commonly referred to as a "rap sheet." The rap sheet identifies the contributor (the local, state, or federal agency that provided the information), the name and physical description of the subject, the date and charge of each arrest, and (sometimes, but not always) dispositions. The FBI also keeps fingerprint cards on people who have been arrested.

What is the National Crime Information Center (NCIC)?

The NCIC primarily serves as a national database available

to all state and local police, containing information on stolen cars and property and on fugitives from justice. When a police officer pulls a car over, he or she will sometimes check the car's license plate number and the driver's license against the NCIC. An increasingly important function of the FBI's NCIC is to serve as an index and clearinghouse for state-held criminal history records, which generally consist of notations of arrest, detention, indictment or other formal criminal charges, and any disposition stemming from those charges (including, for example, dismissal or sentencing).

How does the NCIC work for criminal history data?

As mentioned, state criminal justice agencies are the main keepers of criminal history data. Initially, the FBI hoped that NCIC would be able to maintain criminal histories as well, but the plan was not feasible given the enormous amounts of data and strong political opposition to a national database composed of such sensitive data.

The FBI recently has proposed to create a central index, known as the Interstate Identification Index (III), which would point a state seeking an individual's criminal history to the record system of another state holding the record.

Are arrest and conviction records confidential?

Not really. The data traditionally receiving the most confidential treatment were arrest data not accompanied by a disposition that would show if the arrest led to a conviction, dismissal, etc. Seeking to avoid stigmatizing individuals because of past arrests that did not lead to convictions, forty-seven states have laws that bar release of such data for noncriminal purposes, including employers checking on job applicants.

In addition, the FBI since 1974 has operated under the so-called "one-year rule," which barred dissemination of arrest records older than one year which lack disposition data even to limited, authorized non-law enforcement requesters. The FBI in 1988 proposed dropping that restriction and met with swift criticism from Congress.

For the most part, however, arrest and conviction data are widely available, particularly within the criminal justice system. The main rules governing criminal history data were issued by the federal Law Enforcement Assistance Administration (LEAA). The LEAA regulations apply to the FBI and to state and local agencies that have received LEAA funds for the collection, storage, and dissemination of criminal history records in either manual or automated systems since 1 July 1973. Because LEAA financial assistance has been given to almost all state and local criminal justice records agencies and because the regulations contain many exemptions, their practical effect is limited.

First, the regulations apply only to "criminal history record information," which is defined to consist of notations of arrest, detention, indictment or other formal criminal charges, and any disposition stemming from those charges (including, for example, dismissal or sentencing).[4] Criminal history record information does not include, and therefore the LEAA regulations do not govern, the following:

1. "Wanted" posters;
2. Original records of entry (such as police arrest books or "blotters") that are compiled chronologically and required by law or long standing custom to be made public;
3. Court records;
4. Opinions in public judicial proceedings;
5. Records of traffic offenses maintained for licensing purposes;
6. Announcements of executive clemency;
7. Fingerprint records compiled for use outside the criminal justice system, such as background checks for employment in public agencies.[5]

Even with respect to data defined as criminal history record information, LEAA regulations place no limit on dissemination for criminal justice purposes, including employment within the criminal justice system.[6] Furthermore, the regulations place no limits on the dissemination of criminal history information about an offense for which an individual is currently within the jurisdiction of the criminal justice system.[7] For purposes of this provision, a person is within the system at any time from arrest through incarceration, including parole, probation, or other court-ordered supervision. Moreover, when an agency possesses incomplete records and can obtain no current information indicating whether a person is still within the criminal justice system, it may assume that a person is within the system for a period of one year following the date of arrest.

The LEAA regulations place no limits on the dissemination of conviction information.[8] Unless sealed or otherwise restricted by state law, conviction records can be disseminated to almost anyone. (See the explanation of sealing statutes later in this chapter.)

Thus, the only real restrictions imposed by the LEAA regulations are upon the dissemination of "nonconviction data" to public or private agencies that are not a part of the criminal justice system. "Nonconviction data" include criminal history information when the arrest charges were not referred for prosecution, were dismissed, or resulted in an acquittal. In addition, the category is defined to cover records of arrests more than a year old that are unaccompanied by disposition information and for which no prosecution is actively pending.[9]

The regulations provide that nonconviction data may be disseminated only to:

1. Criminal justice agencies for criminal justice and employment purposes;
2. Public and private agencies authorized by state or federal statute, executive order, local ordinance, or court decision to receive them;
3. Private individuals and agencies acting under contract to a criminal justice agency to provide criminal justice services;
4. Agencies engaged in evaluative or statistical research.[10]

May employers learn about a job applicant's arrests and convictions?

Forty-seven states restrict disclosure of nonconviction data outside of the criminal justice system. LEAA rules similarly bar release of arrest data more than a year old that are not accompanied by dispositions. In the main, though, conviction data are generally available to private employers. Moreover, through separate legislation, Congress has authorized the FBI to disclose criminal history records to federally chartered or insured banks, portions of the securities industry, the commodities industry, the nuclear power industry, and day care centers. And while regulations appear to deny employers access to records of arrests not followed by conviction, they are vague enough to allow such access unless a state statute, regulation, or court ruling explicitly forbids it. A few states— notably California, Illinois, Massachusetts, and New York— forbid employers to ask applicants about arrests that did not result in convictions.[11] But almost everywhere, some or all public agencies may (or even must) check the arrest as well as conviction records of employment applicants, and many state occupational licensing laws require such a check. After law enforcement agencies, employers are the major users of criminal justice records, and an arrest history—even without conviction—is one of the most common factors in employment discrimination.

Do people have a right to see their own arrest and conviction records?

Yes. A person's access to his own criminal justice records is governed by federal and state regulations and, in some states, by statute. A person may obtain a copy of his FBI rap sheet by writing directly to the FBI Identification Division, Washington D.C. 20537. The request must be accompanied by name, date and place of birth, and a set of rolled-ink fingerprint impressions taken upon standard fingerprint cards. A set of fingerprints can be most simply obtained at a local police station upon request.[12]

Each request for an FBI rap sheet must be accompanied by a five dollar fee in the form of a certified check or money order payable to the Treasurer of the United States. A person may request a waiver of the fee based upon a claim of indigency. An indigency application may be made by enclosing a brief letter explaining the reasons why one is unable to pay the fee. If the letter is not acceptable to the FBI, it will usually advise the writer of the problem and give him the opportunity to submit additional information. The FBI will consider, but need not grant, a request to waive the fee.

The rap sheets maintained by state repositories do not necessarily duplicate rap sheets maintained by the FBI. Often there will be significant differences in the information maintained on a person by several different repositories. A person who wishes to inspect his rap sheet is well advised to check both the FBI and the repository of any state in which an arrest took place.

A few states provide a right of access to one's own criminal history records by statute.[13] LEAA regulations require that individuals be given the right of access to their rap sheets in any record system assisted with LEAA funds, although the scope of the right and the procedures for exercising it vary. A telephone call to the criminal records division of local police headquarters should be able to determine what procedure must be followed in one's own state. However, records of arrests and convictions that occurred in other states will seldom be compiled on the rap sheet in one's home state; it is therefore necessary to ask for one's rap sheet from the repository of every state in which an arrest or conviction took place. (Again, a telephone call to the criminal records division of a police department in each of these other states should elicit the necessary instructions for obtaining a rap sheet.)

It is worth repeating this admonition: because the consequences of the use of arrest and conviction information both within the community of criminal justice agencies and outside it—especially by employers—can be so serious, anyone who has ever been arrested or convicted should check his rap sheets wherever they are stored, in state repositories as well as with the FBI. In spite of the trouble and expense, it is important to find out what information the rap sheets contain, to make sure they are complete and correct, and—whenever possible—to seal them or take other steps to prevent their further dissemination.

May a rap sheet be corrected if it contains inaccurate or incomplete information?

Yes. FBI regulations provide that if an individual believes his FBI rap sheet is inaccurate or incomplete, correction or updating of the information must be requested by the police department or other criminal justice agency that contributed the information to the FBI.[14] The FBI will make such changes as are directed by the contributing agency.

Getting a contributing agency to forward a rap-sheet correction to the FBI can be something of an ordeal. Overburdened or uninterested police officials may simply not want to be bothered, and the burden of proof to substantiate the correction—for example, by producing a copy of a court record showing the disposition of an arrest—is usually upon the subject of the record. However, the stakes are well worth the effort; it can be significant, if one has a later encounter with the police or the courts, to show that an earlier arrest actually ended in the dismissal of charges or acquittal. (Disposition information is the most frequently missing or incorrect item.) People who experience difficulties in correcting a record often find they need a lawyer's help, although it can be done alone with persistence and determination.

It is a good idea to ask the police department or other contributing agency to forward a correction to the state respository as well as to the FBI—in fact, anyplace else where the original record was sent. Procedures for correction under statutes or regulations, where they exist, are often similar to those of the FBI and require the correction to be made by the contributing agency. Local legal aid and legal services societies and ex-offender organizations are good sources of information about the procedures to be followed for the correction of a rap sheet in any particular state or locality.

May an arrest or conviction record be sealed or expunged?

Under some circumstances. Nearly half the states provide for the sealing or expungement (erasing) of certain arrest or conviction records by statute. The statutes cover different kinds of records and different sets of circumstances and require various procedures to be initiated by record subjects, the courts, or the state record repository. In New York, for example, records of arrests not resulting in conviction are supposed to be sealed automatically and fingerprints and mug shots returned to the subject. In Massachusetts, a convicted person can petition the court that had jurisdiction of the case to seal the record of a felony conviction after ten years or a misdemeanor conviction after five. In Maryland, the record of an arrest not followed by conviction, or a conviction followed by a sentence of probation, can be expunged upon the defendant's petition to the court. [15] But state sealing and expungement statutes have many loopholes. Often a sealed or even supposedly expunged record remains available for certain purposes: it may be reopened by petition of a prosecutor to a court, for example, or disclosed to gun-licensing or law-enforcement agencies. In some jurisdictions, sealed records may not be sealed or physically sequestered at all but merely stamped with the word "sealed" or placed in a separate but open file.

Sealing or expungement may be barred totally if the person was ever convicted of a crime in another jurisdiction. The sealing procedure may have to be initiated by the defendant, and many defendants remain unaware of their right to seek such relief. In some states, a defendant's petition to seal can be denied if the prosecutor claims that the record should remain open "in the interests of justice."[16] Legal services and ex-offender organizations can provide information on the sealing procedures available in the various states that have sealing or expungement laws.

Where there are no statutes allowing the sealing or expungement of a record, the courts have occasionally stepped in to provide relief to a person who wishes to have an arrest or conviction record destroyed. A milestone decision ordering the destruction of an FBI rap sheet was *Menard v. Saxbe*[17] in which the court stressed the stigma and the potential serious harm to an individual in the continued maintenance and possible dissemination of an inaccurate record. In another important case, the court ordered the destruction of the arrest records of thirteen thousand persons who were illegally arrested during the 1971 antiwar Mayday demonstrations in Washington D.C.[18]

A lawsuit to expunge or even to correct a record can be very difficult. If there is no statutory or regulatory remedy, it is possible that a court will provide relief where an arrest was clearly illegal or where it can be demonstrated that the likely harm to the individual in the dissemination of the records (such as to employers) outweighs the "compelling interest of law enforcement" in maintaining the record. Yet would-be litigants should be cautioned by the decision of the US Supreme Court in *Paul v. Davis* in 1976,[19] which held that the wide public circulation of an arrest record—an erroneous record at that—by police officials did not violate the right of privacy or any other constitutional right.

Are juvenile arrest and conviction records confidential?

Juvenile records are purportedly made confidential by statute in every state. Many states provide procedures by which a juvenile record may be sealed or expunged upon the individual's eighteenth or twenty-first birthday. Nonetheless, records of juvenile arrests and convictions (sometimes called "adjudications of delinquency" in the parlance of the juvenile court) are widely disseminated among criminal justice agencies and beyond—to social services agencies, schools, clinics, and other agencies or institutions that deal with juveniles. In practice, it is not difficult to obtain access to juvenile arrest and conviction records.[20]

One of the most serious problems faced by a person who has a juvenile record is the possibility that it will be discovered by prospective employers. Employers frequently circumvent the statutory barriers that deny them direct access to juvenile records simply by demanding that applicants reveal any juvenile arrests or convictions. While the applicant may be tempted to lie, he knows that the employer may reject him later for dishonesty if the truth comes out. In fact, applications for many jobs with government agencies, and even with some private employers, state specifically that submission of false information on the application will be treated as sufficient reason for rejection or dismissal. There is no answer to this dilemma so long as employers are virtually unrestricted in the questions they may ask applicants.

Can anyone gain access to other people's FBI-held rap sheets under the Freedom of Information Act?

No. Under a 1989 Supreme Court ruling, FBI rap sheets can be witheld under Exemption 7 (C), which safeguards personal privacy in law enforcement records. News media representatives had requested rap sheets of an alleged underworld figure, arguing that since the data were available publicly in local police stations at the time of the arrest, they could not later be considered confidential under the FOIA. However, a unanimous Supreme Court ruled privacy interests outweigh the public's need to see sensitive rap-sheet data. "The substantial character of [the privacy] interest is affected by the fact that in today's society the computer can accumulate and store information that would otherwise have surely been forgotten long before a person attains the age of 80, when the FBI's rap sheets are discarded," said Justice John Paul Stevens.[21]

NOTES

1. 28 U.S.C. § 534.
2. Bureau of Justice Statistics, State Criminal Records Repositories 1 (1985); SEARCH Group, Inc., *Criminal Justice Information Policy: Privacy and the Private Employer.*
3. US Congress, Office of Technology Assessment (OTA), *Alternatives for a National Computerized Criminal History System* 141 (1982).
4. 28 C.F.R. § 20.3 (b).
5. 28 C.F.R. § 20.20 (b) and 20.3 (b).
6. 28 C.F.R. § 20.21 (b) (1).
7. 28 C.F.R. § 20.21 (c).
8. 28 C.F.R. § 20.21 (b).
9. 28 C.F.R. § 20.3 (k).
10. 28 C.F.R. § 20.21 (b) (1)–(4).
11. Cal. Lab. Code § 432.7; Ill. Rev. Stat. ch. 48, para. 853; Mass. Ann. Laws, *supra* note 14; N.Y. Correc. Law 750 *et seq.*
12. 28 C.F.R. § 16.30.
13. *See, e.g.,* Alaska Stat. § 12.62.010; Ark Stat. Ann. § 5-1109; Cal. Penal Code § 11075–81; Ga. Code Ann. § 92A-30006; Iowa Code Ann., *supra* note 10; Me. Rev. Stat. Ann. tit. 16, § 606; Va. Code § 9-111.3.
14. 28 C.F.R. § 16.30.
15. N.Y. Crim Proc. Law, 160.50; Mass. Ann. Laws ch. 276, § 100A–C; Md. Ann. Code art. 27, § 735–41.
16. *E.g.,* N.Y. Crim. Proc. Law, *supra* note 14.
17. 498 F.2d 1017 (D.C. Cir. 1974).
18. *Sullivan v. Murphy,* 478 F2d 938 (D.C. Cir. 1973), *cert. denied,* 414 U.S. 880 (1974).
19. 424 U.S. 693 (1976).
20. *See* Alan Sussman, *The Rights of Young People,* 108–112 (Avon 1977).
21. *U.S. Dept. of Justice v. Reporters Committee for Freedom of Press,* Sup. Ct. No. 87-1379, Mar. 22, 1989.

V

Social Services Records

What kinds of information are contained in social services records?

Every kind of personal information imaginable. Social services records are the personal records maintained by government agencies that dispense cash or services to financially needy persons. Welfare is one form of such assistance. So are food stamps, Medicaid, housing subsidies, employment training, family planning services, drug or alcohol abuse treatment, day care, legal services, rehabilitative services for the handicapped, and dozens of other programs that administer publicly funded assistance and services free or at low cost to people who are in need.

Social services and welfare records contain all the personal information that is initially gathered to determine and verify a client's eligibility for benefits, descriptions of the services and benefits dispensed to the client, and the accumulation of data recording the course of the client's relationship with the agency. In addition to objective data, such records may contain the judgments and observations of agency personnel about a client's character or attitudes. Information about the client's family is frequently included, even though other family members are not receiving benefits. Certain types of records may contain highly sensitive information: the client's personal confidences to a counselor in a drug treatment program, for example, or confessions of criminal offenses to a legal services attorney.

Because publicly funded social services programs run the gamut of human experience and problems, so too do the records they generate.

Must welfare clients and other recipients of government assistance reveal all their personal records in order to establish eligibility for benefits?

Generally, yes. Clients are required not only to produce records in their own possession but also to waive the confidentiality of records held by third parties. Welfare and other social services agencies establish and verify client eligibility primarily by collecting detailed personal information. Subjects covered include clients' finances and possessions, education, employment, criminal history, physical and mental health, family and social relationships, use of drugs and alcohol, sometimes even the intimacies of their sex lives and use of contraceptives. There is no practical way for a prospective client to withhold any of this information from an assistance agency without seriously jeopardizing his efforts to obtain benefits. The client is forced to allow deep intrusions into his personal life as the price for receiving government help.

To establish eligibility for most public assistance and social service programs, the client must sign a waiver of confidentiality permitting the administering agency to examine all his bank, tax, medical, employment, and similar personal records, to exchange information with other agencies that have served the client, and to talk with neighbors, employers, and personal acquaintances. Although other chapters of this book suggest methods by which readers might avoid or at least narrow the scope of such "blanket waivers," there is little chance that the individual public assistance or social services client, acting independently, can successfully do so.

While clients cannot resist most government intrusions into their personal lives and records, there are established procedures whereby the discriminatory or unfair use of certain information to make a decision about a client can be challenged. These procedures vary according to the program in question and the jurisdiction—federal, state, or local—in which it is administered. Local welfare rights and legal services organizations can advise a client of the hearing rights available in a particular social services or welfare program.

Must recipients of assistance allow agency officials into their homes?

Yes. Caseworkers may visit recipients in their homes and conduct "reasonable" searches to assess the client's living conditions. But the Supreme Court has outlawed such "unreasonable" searches as middle-of-the-night surprise visits.[1]

May clients see and correct their records?

Frequently not. Despite the obvious hardships and injustices that result when an agency does not have accurate, timely, complete, and relevant records upon which to base its eligibility judgments, most welfare and social services programs do not provide formal client rights of access and correction.

There are exceptions. When a client has requested a hearing to challenge an agency's decision, he or she is often allowed to examine at least those documents and records the agency will use at the hearing. Clients of the federally funded, state-administered Aid to Families with Dependent Children (AFDC), Medicaid, and Title XX Social Services programs have the right, preparatory to a hearing, to examine their complete case files.[2] Any social services programs administered directly by a federal agency, such as the Supplemental Security Income program of the Social Security Administration, are subject to client rights of access and correction under the Privacy Act of 1974.[3] Records held by state welfare and social services agencies may be open to clients where there is an analogous state privacy act.

However, there are many state and local programs that do not permit client access under any conditions. Moreover, even in those programs in which clients have a right of access preparatory to a hearing, the client who has no grounds for a hearing but merely wishes to inspect his records, to see what is there and whether it is correct, usually has no means of doing so.

With or without formal procedures for access, individual caseworkers will sometimes give the client the chance to review his own records. The client should always explore this possibility. If a request is refused by the caseworker, local welfare rights or legal services organizations can offer guidance on rights of access and correction in specific welfare and social services programs.

May agencies disclose information from case records without a client's permission?

Usually, yes. Most welfare and social services programs are subject to statutes or regulations that require, in general terms, that the confidentiality of client records must be protected. These requirements, however, are hedged by vague language and numerous exceptions. For example, an agency is nearly always permitted to make disclosures "necessary to provide service to the individual" or "for purposes directly connected to the program." Such standards allow disclosures not only to other agencies presently serving the client, but also to agencies that may serve the client in the future, even when he has not initiated an application. Many states, as well as counties, localities, and federal agencies, operate central "human services" data banks to which client records are submitted for virtually permanent storage. Police and other criminal justice officials can often obtain information from client records simply on request. Schools, employers, and landlords are sometimes told that a student, employee, or tenant is the client of a welfare or social services program. Records are often made available to researchers. So loose are the confidentiality regulations for most programs that these disclosures are perfectly legal. On the other hand, some programs maintain very strict confidentiality; for example, federally funded drug and alcohol abuse treatment programs generally protect client records even against a subpoena.[4]

Disclosures of client records often occur under procedures designed to combat fraud—to catch "welfare cheats." Government auditors are frequently empowered to examine individual client records to insure that both eligibility determinations and provisions of services are in accordance with applicable law and regulations. On a larger scale are audits implemented by computer matches of separate record systems; for example, the matching of the names of welfare clients against employment rolls to find welfare recipients who are earning money in violation of eligibility rules. Inspired by the federal government's Project Match, launched in 1977, which matched the federal payroll against local welfare rolls, many states and localities have instituted similar computerized record-matching operations involving both public and private payrolls (see chapter 1 on government information practices).

Except where client records are directly subject to the confidentiality provisions of the federal Privacy Act or a state privacy act, the welfare or social services client has no meaningful legal "expectation of privacy" and no practical recourse when a disclosure is made without his or her permission.

Has data sharing by social service agencies become more systematic?

Yes, and the Internal Revenue Service's role is now institutionalized. The Deficit Reduction Act (DEFRA) of 1984 required agencies distributing social welfare benefits to engage in "front-end verification" of applicants' income to determine their eligibility for the program. This led in 1986 to the creation of the State Income Eligibility Verification Systems (SIEVS), which contains wage and benefit data from state wage information collection agencies, as well as benefit and other income data from the US Social Security Administration and unearned income data from the IRS. Because SIEVS entails on-line linkage of state and federal databases, a congressional study called it a "*de facto* national data base."[5]

What's in store for the future?

Federal planners are eyeing the possibility of instituting a kind of US "credit card" or "smart card" for recipients of Medicaid, welfare, food stamps, and other benefits. The plastic identity card would instantly debit a recipient's account, necessitating creation of a central program database in order to calculate benefits. In fact, a pilot program is in effect for food stamps. "Most of the present data linkages occur within the public sector," said the Office of Technology Assessment, a congressional research arm. But the proposed smart card system would bring fundamental changes by linking public databases to private ones. OTA said:

> Medical information supplied by doctors and hospitals could then become part of that database. Medical insurers would be part of the communication link in order to certify that Medicaid clients had exhausted their private coverage. Food stores could also be part of such a national database, providing information on buying habits of millions of Americans. Changes of this nature could increase the surveillance capabilities of the national database. These changes might also change public perceptions of privacy protection.

> A decentralized database would be contained in the card's memory in order to execute transactions. The need for both a centralized and decentralized database, and periodic linkages between them for updating data, will require new procedures to ensure privacy and security.

What is the Parent Locator Service?

It is a record-searching operation implementing the Child Support Enforcement Program under Title IV-D of the Social Security Act.[6] Its purpose is to locate the absent parent of children receiving AFDC benefits and to collect child-support payments from them as a full or partial substitute for public assistance. The federal government gives special grants to states that establish child support enforcement agencies and parent locator services; in addition, the federal government itself operates a Parent Locator Service (PLS) within the Department of Health and Human Services.

Parents who are recipients of AFDC must, as a condition of benefits, cooperate with the PLS to find an absent parent. This means that in most cases, a woman must name the father of her children, cooperate in establishing paternity, and give information that will help to determine his whereabouts. If she refuses, she will lose her benefits, and the benefits for her children will be paid to and administered by a third party. There is a "good cause" exception, which exempts the mother from these requirements if efforts to locate the missing father would not be in the "best interests" of the child. Such a determination might be made if the child was conceived by rape or incest or if it is reasonably anticipated that the father would harm the child or the mother, physically or emotionally. But even to establish "good cause," the mother must give information about the identity of the father and the nature of their relationship. In some states, PLS paternity investigations have required women to complete questionnaires revealing all of their sexual relationships and to take polygraph tests.

The PLS is also available, on a voluntary basis, to parents who are not on welfare, to force an absent father to pay court-awarded child support payments.

The PLS is a cooperative federal-state enterprise. Tax, welfare, motor-vehicle, post office, police, in fact any records of any federal, state, or local government agency may be searched for clues to the whereabouts of the absent parent, and so may the records of private organizations, such as employers, unions, and telephone companies. The key to the search is usually the Social Security number, which has come to be used as the universal identifier for all important public and private records. The authority of a PLS agency to search through records usually overrides other regulatory or statutory protection for the confidentiality of records. Except in the few states that have privacy acts, the confidentiality of the records compiled by state PLS and child support enforcement agencies themselves is protected only by agency regulations. As is the case with so many other social services records, these regulations give record subjects no legally enforceable expectation of confidentiality to protect them against unauthorized disclosures. It must be emphasized that the subjects of PLS records need not themselves be public assistance clients; they need only be named as an absent parent by a person who is a public assistance client.

NOTES

1. *Wyman v. James*, 400 U.S. 309 (1971).
2. 45 C.F.R. § 205.10(a)(13)(i).
3. 5 U.S.C. § 552a.
4. 42 C.F.R. § 2.1–2.67.
5. Office of Technology Assessment, *Electronic Delivery of Public Assistance Benefits: Technology Options and Policy Issues* (Background Paper, 1988).
6. 42 U.S.C. §§ 402(a), 454(4), 602(a)(26), 654(4), as amended by Pub. L. No. 93–647 and Pub. L. No. 94-88; 45 C.F.R. §§ 232 and 302.

VI
Social Security Numbers

Is the Social Security number a universal identifier?

Not technically, but the Social Security number (SSN) is so widely used as an identifier by both government and private agencies that many people consider it to be a *de facto* national identifier. To be a true universal identifier, a label would have to be unique to each person: no more than one person would have a given number, and no person would have more than one number. A person would carry the same number throughout his life, and it would not be reused after his death. It would contain internal check features so that errors in transcription or communication could be detected easily. The SSN does not meet these criteria. Many people have more than one number. Some numbers have been issued to or used by more than one person. The SSN does not contain any internal check features, and it can be deliberately falsified or inadvertently misreported.[1] But these technical deficiencies have not prevented widespread reliance on the SSN for authentication and identification purposes. The number is popularly accepted and treated as a universal identifier.

Why is a universal identifier a threat to the right of privacy?

The use of a common label to identify the records of individuals in many separate record systems makes it easier, cheaper, and therefore more practical to exchange, compare, and combine information among those various systems. This, in turn, makes it easier for government agencies and private organizations to trace any individual from cradle to grave and thus encloses each person ever more tightly in a "record prison," unable to escape the past or protect any aspect of his or her life from scrutiny. It must be emphasized that the absence of a universal identifier will not by itself prevent the pooling and linking of records, particularly with today's sophisticated computer technology, nor does the use of a universal identifier by itself cause record linking. The availability of a universal identifier simply makes such linking easier and therefore more likely to occur. An example of a particularly wide-ranging record-linking project through use of the SSN is the comparison of employment, unemployment compensation, Social Security, and welfare records under Project Match, described in chapter 1.

Another danger of the universal identifier is that it gives impetus to the development of a mandatory national identity document. If each person has a single number that can be used to identify and authenticate all of his records, an identity card would be a handy means of establishing not only his identity but also his entitlement to certain benefits and privileges. A familiar example is the recurring proposal for an identity card to be carried by all citizens and resident aliens who are legally entitled to hold a job in the United States, a device intended to discourage the employment of undocumented ("illegal") aliens. The confiscation, or even the threat of confiscation, of such a document would be a formidable means of controlling people's behavior. The demand to "show one's papers" has long been regarded as the hallmark of a police state.

A third danger is the likelihood that a national population register would probably become necessary to authenticate the universal identifier. To prevent forgery, fraud, and bureaucratic error, the information on an identity card would have to be verifiable through comparison with a population register. Such a register could easily become the basis for a national databank—the much feared "one big dossier" compiled and maintained on each individual from birth to death.

What kinds of record systems use the SSN as an identifier?

The original use of the SSN, of course, was to number personal accounts for the collection of taxes and payment of benefits in the Social Security program. The first numbers were assigned in 1936. A year later, it was decided that the same identifier should be used to number accounts in state unemployment-insurance systems. In 1943, Executive Order 9397 was issued by President Roosevelt authorizing any federal agency to use the SSN for new data systems requiring permanent account numbers on records pertaining to individuals. This authority was not used for many years, even by the federal Civil Service Commission, for whose benefit it was originally intended.

In 1961, the Internal Revenue Service decided to designate the SSN as the taxpayer identification number. Thereafter, new uses by government agencies followed in rapid succession: for Treasury bonds, for old-age-assistance benefits accounts, for state and federal civil-service employee records, for Veterans' Administration hospital records, for Indian Health Service patient records, as the military-personnel service number, for customer records in bank and securities transactions, for motor vehicle registration and driver's licenses in many states, and for client records (including those of children) in local, state, and federal public assistance programs.

Under the Tax Reform Act of 1976, Congress granted states permission to use the SSN for motor vehicle registration records and driver's licenses. Currently some three dozen states use the SSN as a driver identification number. The 1976 law also authorized SSN use for the administration of local and state tax laws and of general public assistance (welfare) programs and for implementation of the Parent Locator Service.

In 1984, Congress again expanded required uses of the Social Security number when it enacted the Deficit Reduction Act of 1984. The law required all people with bank accounts to provide their Social Security numbers to their banks so IRS computers could match the amount of interest reported by taxpayers with the amounts reported to the IRS by banks. The law also required recipients of federal benefits — and in many cases their households — to provide social service agencies with their Social Security numbers. (More recently the 1986 Tax Reform Act requires parents to show Social Security numbers for children over 5 who are claimed as dependents.)

In addition to banks, the SSN is used frequently in such private industries as insurance, department store charge accounts and credit card accounts, telephone and utility company accounts, student identification numbers, library cards, and membership records in labor unions and professional associations. Outside the financial area, private organizations do not have legal authority to demand your Social Security number. But most people are so conditioned into disclosing it that few people differentiate between those who are authorized to have it and those who are not.

What can people do who are concerned about guarding their Social Security number?

If the demand comes from a government agency, the person should not comply until the agency meets its obligations under the Privacy Act of 1974 to (1) cite its formal legal authority for using the number, (2) reveal whether disclosure is mandatory or voluntary, (3) explain how the number will be used. Unless the number will be used for records of taxes, motor vehicle registration, driver's licenses, or general public assistance, or for implementation of the Parent Locator System, the agency's legal authority to use the number must predate 1 January 1975.[2]

If the demand comes from a private agency or business and is not required for governmental purposes, the individual should stand his ground as long as possible and, if he or she cares enough, take his business elsewhere. That, of course, may not be easy, as more and more private organizations use the SSN for their record systems.

Will the courts support a person's refusal to disclose his SSN?

Not usually. One case that went to the US Supreme Court involved a Native American, Stephen J. Roy, who challenged, on religious grounds, the requirement that welfare recipients provide their children's SSNs. Roy said his daughter, Little Bird of the Snow, was entitled to Aid to Families with Dependent Children (AFDC) but that he did not want to obtain an SSN for her because such a number would "rob" her of her spirit and was in violation of their religious beliefs. A federal judge in Pennsylvania agreed, and said the government could accommodate her religious beliefs and still grant public assistance. But the Supreme Court reversed. The majority ruled that detecting fraud was a compelling government interest and that use of the Social Security number, which was mandated by Congress, was the key to such detecting.

Summarizing the SSN's evolution, Justice Rehnquist wrote, "Social Security numbers are unique numerical identifiers and are used pervasively in these programs. The numbers are used, for example, to keep track of persons no longer entitled to receive food stamps because of past fraud or abuses of the program. Moreover, the existence of this unique numerical identifier creates opportunties for ferreting out fraudulent applications through computer 'matching' techniques."[3]

In a 1977 case, a federal court in New York upheld the refusal of a family of welfare recipients to obtain SSNs for their children, accepting the parents' assertions of their "sincerely held" religious belief that the enumeration is a "mark of the Beast" and "device of the Antichrist" forbidden by the Bible. The court in this case deferred to the plaintiffs' objectons on First Amendment grounds of religious freedom and did not venture into broader questions of the constitutional right of privacy of welfare recipients as a class, as the Supreme Court did later in the *Roy* case.[4]

There have also been some successful instances of resistance to demands for SSNs where litigation was threatened or filed but not concluded. In response to persistent pressure by ACLU affiliates, the California Bar Association, for example, dropped its requirement for the submission of an SSN by a candidate for admission; the number was removed from fishing licenses in Maine; and several state university systems ended their requirements that SSNs be submitted by students.

In general, the person who wishes to challenge what appears to be an improper use of the SSN by a public agency should not expect the courts to do more than examine existing state and federal statutes to determine whether they are being properly applied in the given circumstances. At present it does not seem likely that the courts will question the judgment of the legislatures on the SSN or explore the constitutional principles raised by the use of a universal identifier.

Is the federal government permitted to disclose Social Security numbers (SSNs) to private institutions?

Although that question cannot be answered definitively, a

controversy that arose in April of 1989 may ultimately lead Congress or the courts to establish a new SSN disclosure policy. The dispute centered on a Social Security Administration program to verify SSNs for credit bureaus between 1984 and 1988 that was never reported to Congress. Under the program, the SSA received magnetic tapes from Citicorp and TRW with names and SSNs, matched them against its database, and informed the companies which names and numbers did not square with SSA records. The agency did not supply the correct names or numbers. For Citicorp, the SSA carried out the "negative verification" program for three million records. In the first run, a check of 932,610 numbers revealed an astounding 423,610 "unverified" or incorrect numbers.

Similarly a check of 151,953 TRW records found 42,860 were unverifiable. In 1989 the SSA was gearing up to check TRW's entire database of 140 million names and SSNs, but the plan was abruptly halted after it was leaked to Congress and exposed in the press.

TRW initially sought SSA participation in the scheme in 1979 and 1980 but was rejected on both occasions because Carter administration officials concluded that strong privacy interests made it improper for the SSA to encourage expanded use of SSNs. It was not clear when or by whom in the Reagan administration the decision was reversed. In a 1988 legal opinion, SSA Chief Counsel Donald Gonya said that since the FOIA might permit disclosure of SSNs, the Privacy Act did not prohibit it.

However, the Congressional Research Service (CRS) concluded the scheme violated the Privacy Act, which bars agencies from disclosing any records "by any means of communication to any person" without his or her consent or without authorization by an exception. The CRS said the government's FOIA arguments did not hold because courts have upheld the right to neither confirm nor deny records and that a requester's commercial interest in otherwise private data cannot outweigh privacy interests. After the SSA plan was exposed, Public Citizen, a Ralph Nader organization said it was considering a Privacy Act lawsuit against the government.[5]

NOTES

1. For other attributes of a standard identifier and the failure of the SSN to meet those requirements, see Secretary's Advisory Committee on Automated Personal Data Systems, US Department of Health, Education, and Welfare, *Records, Computers and the Rights of Citizens*, chapter 7 (July 1973).
2. Pub. L. No. 93-579, p. 7.
3. *Bowen v. Roy*, 776 U.S. 693 (1986).
4. *Stevens v. Berger*, 428 F. Supp. 896 (E.D.N.Y. 1977).
5. *Privacy Times*, Apr. 26, 1989.

VII

Electronic Communications

The twentieth century has witnessed a revolution in communications systems and technologies. The telephone, initially a device for a privileged few, became a household item. The benefits to individuals, families, businesses, and government seemed endless. One benefit for the police, as well as for others who had the resources, was a newfound ability to eavesdrop, or wiretap, phone conversations.

The computer age had an equally dramatic impact. Telephone technology itself improved so that microwave transmissions streamlined the old fashioned "wire system." Moreover, the marriage of telephones and computers meant that data could be beamed from terminal to terminal, across the street or to the other side of the world. By the 1980s, reams of sensitive data, including trade secrets, personal health information, and financial data regularly entered the stream of telephone communications and were stored in computers.

The ramifications for privacy are profound. Technology has advanced to the point where virtually any phone conversation or any data transmission can be intercepted. In fact, the National Security Agency, the federal government's most secret body, was created to intercept communications.[1]

In 1923 the US Supreme Court held that wiretapping did not violate the Fourth Amendment since there was no searching, no seizure of anything tangible, no physical trespass.[2] Forty years later, the Court reversed itself, ruling in two cases that the Fourth Amendment protected against warrantless interception of telephone conversations and electronic eavesdropping of oral conversation.[3] Congress too recognized the need for statutory privacy protection, albeit a bit later. In 1968 it passed the Omnibus Crime Control and Safe Streets Act, including Title III,[4] which restricted wiretapping. In 1986, recognizing that advances in technology required updating the law, Congress approved and President Reagan signed the Electronic Communications Privacy Act (ECPA).[5]

How did the 1968 Title III law restrict wiretapping?

Designed to bolster the Fourth Amendment's guarantees against unreasonable searches, it required the government to obtain a court order before wiretapping a "wire communication" (ordinarily a phone conversation) or otherwise eavesdropping on an "oral conversation" during which the parties would have an "expectation of privacy." However, the law allowed the president, consistent with constitutional restrictions, to intercept calls without a warrant in order to obtain foreign intelligence data deemed essential to national security, to protect the nation against potential attack or other hostile acts, including the overthrow of the government. The law restricted government applications for wiretaps to the US Attorney General or a specially designated assistant attorney general, thus centralizing responsibility and the implementation of policy.

The government could wiretap only in the course of investigating certain "designated offenses," including national security offenses (espionage, treason, sabotage, and nuclear secrets); intrinsically serious offenses (murder, kidnapping, riots, and drug-related offenses); and organized crime-style offenses.

Under Title III, the government had to show a court with specificity why it needed the wiretap. The court could deny the application if the government failed to show probable cause, the length of the surveillance, or that normal investigative techniques were inadequate. Once granted, the government was obligated to minimize intrusiveness by listening in only to conversations that were related to the investigation at hand. All this was intended to implement the Fourth Amendment requirement that warrants show sufficient "particularity." This includes;

1. the identity of the person, if known, whose communications are to be intercepted;
2. the nature and location of the communications facilities for which, or the place where, authority to intercept is granted;
3. a particular description of the types of communications sought to be intercepted, and a statement of the particular offense to which it relates;

4. the identity of the agency authorized to intercept the communications, and of the person authorizing the application;
5. the period of time during which such interception is authorized, including a statement as to whether or not the interception shall automatically terminate when the described communications have been first obtained.

The government was supposed to notify those who were the targets of wiretaps, but the notice requirements were vague and did not include notice to people who were not targets but whose conversations may have been overheard.

The government generally was required to record conversations it overheard, and transcripts could be shared with other law enforcers when necessary to establish probable cause for an arrest or search or to develop witnesses. Individuals could sue those who violated the act and seek fines not less than $100 for each day of violation or $1,000, whichever is higher. In addition, an individual could suppress the use of evidence the government collected through an illegal wiretap. Private individuals were barred from intercepting communications; penalties for violations were a $10,000 fine and five years' imprisonment.

What led Congress to amend the law in 1986?

The advance of computer technology and the rapid use of phone systems for electronic mail and other computer-to-computer data transmissions revealed that there were glaring holes in the 1968 law.

The legislative movement received its impetus in 1984 when Senator Patrick Leahy (D-VT), one of the Senate's leading privacy advocates, asked the Justice Department whether the federal wiretap law covered interceptions of electronic mail or computer-to-computer communications. The department replied that it generally did not because the law's outdated definitions limited a person's "reasonable expectation of privacy" to "aural" phone chats, that is, those conversations that could be heard. The department said, "In this rapidly developing area of communications which ranges from cellular non-wire telephone connections to microwave-fed computer terminals, distinctions such as [whether there does or does not exist a reasonable expectation of privacy] are not always clear or obvious."[6]

The Senate Judiciary Committee said in a report accompanying legislation: "The law must advance with the technology to ensure the continued vitality of the fourth amendment. Privacy cannot be left solely on physical protection, or it will gradually erode as technology advances. Congress must act to protect the privacy of our citizens. If we do not, we will promote the gradual erosion of this precious right."[7]

How did the 1986 law cure this problem?

It simply extended Title III's safeguards against unwarranted interception to "non-aural communications," thereby protecting electronic mail and other data transmissions. The law expanded these protections by barring government officials from obtaining data held by a communications company, such as MCI, without a warrant that met the probable cause standard.

What else did the law cover?

It created procedures, parallel to those in the Right to Financial Privacy Act, regulating government access to long distance toll records. Under the Supreme Court's decision in *Smith v. Maryland*,[8] toll records are not protected by the Constitution from government snooping since they belong to the phone company, not the individual customer. The ECPA bolstered confidentiality for toll records by requiring the government to show it "had reason to believe the records would be relevant to a legitimate law enforcement investigation" before they could obtain them. The provisions also require that notice be given to the customer and that he or she have a chance to challenge the government's access. However, notice can be delayed if it would risk flight from prosecution or jeopardize an ongoing investigation.

Unauthorized access to stored electronic communications is punishable by up to one year imprisonment and a $250,000 fine for a first offender if the offense is committed for private or commercial gain or for malicious destruction. In all other cases the fine is limited to not more than $5,000 and imprisonment for not more than six months.

Did the new law keep requirements to minimize monitoring of communications that were not relevant to an authorized investigation?

Yes. In fact, the law extended "minimization" rules to electronic communications. A Senate report said "common sense" dictated that law enforcement officials would delete all nonrelevant materials and disseminate to other officials only that data which were relevant to the investigation.[9]

Are all types of phone conversations protected from interception?

No. Because "radio" communications are easy to monitor, the law does not protect the "radio portion" of cordless phone conversations. This means that anyone can intercept transmissions between the cordless handset and the base unit. However, the "wire portion," from the base unit throughout the regular telephone system is still protected.

How about cellular telephones?

Cellular telephones, most commonly used in cars, employ a technology that makes intentional monitoring more difficult. Moreover, at least part of cellular communications are carried through the wire portion of the phone system. Accordingly, they are protected from interception by the ECPA. However, because cellular conversations are easier to pick up by radio scanners than regular phone communications, the law changed the 1968 interception standard from "willful" to "intentional" so that "inadvertent" interceptions were no longer illegal. This meant that a radio scanner enthusiast who accidentally picked up part of a cellular conversation would not be guilty of violating the law.

Considering the other pressures on it, why was Congress willing to devote so much time and energy to rewriting one of the most complex privacy laws?

There were several factors. First, it was a clear-cut case of old legal protections becoming obsolete because of technological advances. Second, Senators Patrick Leahy and Charles Mathias, Representatives Robert Kastenmeier and Carlos Moorhead, and others readily provided the necessary leadership. Third, the bill had support from a broad-based coalition, coordinated mainly by the American Civil Liberties Union Project on Privacy and Technology, which included the major industry associations and corporations like AT&T, IBM, and the major broadcasting companies. Fourth, it was supported by the federal law enforcement community.

Why did law enforcers endorse the measure?

Because it expanded the number of US Justice Department officials that were authorized to apply for wiretap warrants, thus removing an administrative bottleneck, and it expanded the number of crimes that would warrant wiretaps.

What about intelligence and counterintelligence operations?

Interception of communication for foreign intelligence purposes is exempt from the ECPA. Instead, such activities remained within the exclusive jurisdiction of the Foreign Intelligence Surveillance Act of 1978, which set up a special— and secret—court to review intelligence wiretap applications.

In terms of FBI foreign counterintelligence operations, the bill authorized mandatory FBI access to telephone toll records and electronic communications transactional records (which had been barred by some state public regulatory bodies). But it established a new requirement that the FBI director certify to the communications company that the bureau had reason to believe the information was relevant to an authorized foreign counterintelligence probe.

Does the ECPA prohibit all forms of electronic eavesdropping?

No. Under the "one party consent rule," a person can secretly record telephone and other conversations. According to a 1988 study, an increasing number of Americans are clandestinely eavesdropping on each other, particularly in domestic disputes.[10] Rudolph Brewington, a coauthor of the report, claimed that his ex-wife placed a voice-activated tape recorder under her bed and then staged a sexual assault, apparently to improve her leverage in a divorce suit. Brewington has sued his ex-wife, as well as Radio Shack, the producer of the tape recorder, for invasion of privacy and other torts. The suit, which has forced Radio Shack to admit for the first time that its officials were aware its voice-activated tape recorder could be used for illegal purposes, was pending in a Pennsylvania court at the beginning of 1989.

Brewington's research uncovered nine examples of surreptitious surveillance arising from domestic disputes or jealousy between 1986 and 1988. They involve bugs on telephones, tracking devices, and hidden voice-activated tape recorders. Brewington's study noted that self-help divorce guides are instructing disgruntled mates to take advantage of low-cost surveillance devices and loopholes in the law. Consequently, business is booming.

Brewington expressed hope that Congress and state legislatures would respond with stronger anti-surveillance laws.

Have there been any examples of illegal wiretapping during the 1980s?

Yes. The most prominent cases have been in Cincinnati, where local police and Cincinnati Bell security officials conspired to place as many as 1,200 illegal wiretaps on congressmen, local politicians, businessmen, a major defense contractor, then President Gerald Ford, journalists, and political activists. The case is being investigated by a federal grand jury in Cincinnati. But questionable tactics and the lack of progress by the U.S. attorney's office prompted Senator Patrick Leahy, in July of 1989, to ask Attorney General Richard Thornburgh to review the matter. Thornburgh did not reply before this book went to press. Moreover, several targets of the illegal wiretaps had civil damages lawsuits pending against Cincinnati Bell and the local police.[11]

Allegations of illegal wiretapping in the 1980s also surfaced in Pittsburgh, New Haven, Long Island, Hagerstown (Md.), Sacramento, and Los Angeles, according to the *Privacy Times* newsletter.[12]

NOTES

1. Bamford, James, *Puzzle Palace*. New York: Houghton Mifflin (1982).
2. *Olmstead v. U.S.* 277 U.S. 438 (1929).

3. *Katz v. U.S.* 389 U.S. 347 (1967) and *Berger v. New York* 388 U.S. 41 (1967).

4. 18 U.S.C. 2510–2520.

5. 18 U.S.C.

6. Report of the Senate Judiciary Committee, *Electronic Communications Privacy Act of 1986*, Oct. 17, 1986, p. 4.

7. *Ibid*, p. 5.

8. (*Smith* case) *Smith v. Maryland* 442 U.S. 735 (1979).

9. *Electronic Communications*, p. 31

10. Rudolph Brewington and Robert Moore Jr., Domestic Surveillance: America's Dirty Little Secret (unpublished manuscript, 1988).

11. *Privacy Times*, July 24, 1989.

12. *Id*.

VIII

School Records

What kinds of information are contained in school records?

Much more than just grades. School records describe students' emotional development, social behavior, medical problems, learning problems, political and religious preferences, family members, physical appearance, hobbies and extracurricular interests, ethnic background, economic circumstances, attitudes toward teachers and other students, psychological test scores, criminal history, even personal secrets confided to a friendly teacher or counselor. Their contents range from such objective information as a student's height and weight to the subjective impressions of a teacher about the "tendencies" of an unruly child.

Many people attend school from the time they are three or four years old until their mid-twenties and even beyond. Records generated by each school follow the student and are likely to determine how the student is evaluated and placed by every new teacher and institution in turn. The records maintained on a kindergarten child may some day have an effect on his admission to college or acceptance for employment. Because school records are so influential and so long-lived, it is important that parents and students know what they contain and who has access to them.

Do students have a right to see their own school records?

Yes, if a student is either eighteen years old or attends college, university, or other postsecondary institution and if the school receives federal money from the US Office of Education. The student's right of access is mandated by a federal statute enacted in 1974, the Family Educational Rights and Privacy Act (FERPA), known also as the Buckley amendment.[1] In some localities, state laws, formal state or local school board policies, or the administrative policies of individual schools may give students under eighteen a right of access to some or all of their education records.

The right of access and other rights conferred by the FERPA

do not apply to students at private institutions nor do they apply to students at schools receiving all kinds of federal aid. Only schools that get federal funds through a program administered by the US commissioner of education are obligated to comply with FERPA. A list of such programs is published each year and can be obtained from any regional office of the US Department of Education. The designated programs include some that make loans and grants directly to students which are then paid to the school for educational services.[2]

Do parents have a right to see their children's school records?

Yes. If a student is under eighteen and attends an elementary or secondary school that receives US Office of Education funds, his or her parents are given the right of access under the FERPA to their student's records. When the student becomes an "eligible student" within the definition of the statute—turns eighteen or enters a postsecondary educational institution—rights of access and other rights under the FERPA are automatically transferred from the parents to the student.

Do students have a right to see records maintained by schools they no longer attend?

Yes. But FERPA rights of access do not cover a person who applied for admission but was not accepted.[3] A person turned down for admission to a college does not have a statutory right to see the material in the admission file and so may not be able to learn why he or she was rejected.

How do students and parents know what kinds of records are being kept?

Each school subject to the FERPA must make available to parents and student, on request, a listing of the types and locations of the personal record systems it maintains, together with the titles and addresses of the officials responsible for each system of records.[4]

Do students and their parents have the right to see all of their records?

No. Some records may be withheld. FERPA rights of access

do not cover so-called "desk-drawer notes," the informal notes about students kept by teachers and other school personnel solely for their own use, as long as these are not accessible or revealed to any other person except an official substitute teacher or administrator. Nor do they cover records kept by a campus security force, provided that (1) such records are separately maintained and used only for law-enforcement purposes; (2) they are not disclosed to anyone except law enforcement officials in the jurisdiction (e.g., the local police); and (3) the school's security personnel do not have access to the student's other school records.[5]

Students who are eighteen years or older or who attend a college or other postsecondary institution do not have a right of direct access to medical or psychiatric records, as long as these were created and maintained solely for treatment purposes and are not disclosed to anyone other than individuals providing treatment. These records may, however, be released to a physician of the student's choice—who is then free, of course, to show them to the student. Such records are available to the parent of elementary and secondary students under eighteen.[6]

FERPA rights of access do not allow postsecondary students to see their parent's financial statements, such as statements submitted in applications for scholarship aid. They do not allow students to see confidential letters of recommendation filed before 1 January 1975, as long as these are used only for their originally intended purpose. (If a letter filed before that date, originally used for college admission, is later used for another purpose, such as employment, the student may see it.) And finally, students may not have access to letters of recommendation filed after 1 January 1975 with respect to which they have formally waived their rights of access.[7]

How—and why—do students waive their rights of access to confidential letters of recommendation?

In its original form, the FERPA would have allowed eligible students or their parents to see all letters of recommendation written on their behalf by teachers and others for use in applications for college or graduate school admission, fellowships, special educational programs, employment, etc. The prospect that these traditionally secret letters would be revealed to students alarmed some professional educators so that they lobbied to have the law amended. Advocates on the other side argued that because these letters are so influential in making decisions, particularly for college and graduate school admissions, and because they frequently contain derogatory, misleading, or altogether false information, it is essential that students retain the right to see them. Congress compromised, amending the law to preserve the confidentiality of letters filed before 1 January 1975 and allow a voluntary waiver of the student's right of access to letters filed after that date.

A waiver of access must be in writing. It must be signed by an eligible student or by a parent—unless the student is an applicant for admission to a postsecondary institution, in which case the student must personally execute the waiver, even if he or she is under eighteen. An educational institution may not require a waiver as a condition of admission, financial aid, or any service or benefit. The student must be given, on request, the name of every person who provides a confidential letter. A waiver is valid only so long as a letter of recommendation is used for its originally intended purpose: admission to an educational institution, employment, or the receipt of an honor or honorary recognition. It may be revoked at any time, with respect to new uses of a letter already filed or new letters filed after the date of revocation, and an eligible student may revoke a waiver previously executed by the parent. The waiver must specify the categories of records to which it applies and their intended uses: the student may not be asked to sign a blanket waiver of all rights of access.[8]

Despite these apparently rigorous safeguards, the waiver provision is one of the most commonly abused sections of the FERPA. There have been records of blatant coercion: e.g., the high school guidance counselor who refuses to process any college application unless the student signs a waiver. More frequent, though, is the subtle coercion imposed by the advice given to students that their college applications will not be seriously considered unless they waive their right to see letters of recommendation. Some college and graduate school administrators have perpetuated the tradition of secrecy by insisting that only confidential letters can be "frank," and many application forms contain a bland statement instructing the student to "sign below" to waive your right of access to letters of recommendation. It is very difficult for an individual, especially a young person, to withstand this kind of pressure. Unless the law is changed, or until the academic community changes its own thinking, students may be pushed into signing waivers against their own better judgment. But it should always be remembered that an institution cannot require a waiver, and the student is always entitled to refuse.

How do students and their parents get to see school records?

Each institution is allowed to set its own procedures for the inspection of records. The FERPA requires that the school notify students and their parents annually about their rights under the FERPA and about the procedures to be followed for inspecting records. (Elementary and secondary schools must "provide for the need to effectively notify parents of students identified as having a primary or home language other than English.")[9] Occasionally this is done by mail, more often by notice on a bulletin board or publication in a student handbook or newspaper. But frequently it is not done at all.

The institution must comply with a request for access "within a reasonable period of time," but no longer than forty-five days[10] Furthermore, it must respond to a "reasonable" request for an explanation or interpretation of the material in the record.[11] It may not forbid the eligible student or parent to read the record or to take notes. If a record contains information on students other than the one requesting access, the institution may remove or segregate that information, but where this cannot be done, the pertinent parts of the record may be read to the student or parent orally. No fee may be charged to search for or retrieve a student's records.[12] In some institutions, it may be possible for students to inspect all of their records at once, especially if advance notice has been given to allow officials to gather the records in one place. But the law does not require this, and the student may have to visit several different offices and follow different procedures. Educational institutions have been notably lax about publishing, or even formulating, procedures for inspecting records, a failure that may cause much delay and confusion.

It is important to make a note of everything that happens in the course of attempting to examine one's school records: the date of the request for access, the date of the school's response, the date the records were examined, what records were seen, what records were withheld and the school's reasons for withholding them, any misinformation found in the records, and the names of the officials who handled each step of the process. These facts can be significant in subsequent enforcement proceedings.

May students and parents obtain copies of a record?

Yes. If their inability to obtain copies would effectively deprive them of their rights of access.[13] There are at least two circumstances in which the right to obtain copies could be crucial. The first is inaccessibility: when a former student is far away from the institution or a working parent is unable to make a personal visit during school hours. The second is unwieldiness: when the records are so copious or complex that visual inspection or even taking notes is not sufficient. In either circumstance, the institution must provide copies. In practice, many institutions make copies simply on request. The institution may charge for copies, but only if the fee would not "effectively prevent the parents and students from exercising their right to inspect and review" the records.[14] This suggests that fees may have to be waived altogether for poor families or reduced where it is necessary for the student to obtain large quantities of documents. Each institution must have a published schedule of fees for copies, available to parents and students on request.[15]

If a record contains inaccurate information, can it be changed?

Yes. A parent or eligible student may ask the school to amend any information on the grounds that it is inaccurate, misleading, or in violation of the student's right of privacy or other rights. Within a reasonable period of time, the institution must decide whether or not to comply. If it refuses, it must inform the parent or student of the right to a hearing.[16]

The scope of the right to challenge inaccurate or misleading information, or information that violates the student's rights, is only vaguely defined. The legislative history of the FERPA is clear on at least one point: the provision is not applicable to a student's grades.[17] A student may not use the FERPA to challenge the teacher's judgment in deciding what grade to give for a course. However, a student may challenge the accuracy of the record in reporting the grade actually received — e.g., if the record shows a *B* when an *A* was usually received.

There are no generally accepted standards for determining what kinds of information would violate a student's privacy or other rights. The FERPA itself addresses only the procedures by which an educational institution maintains and disseminates student records; it does not deal with the substantive content of the records. The student or parent who wants to challenge information on the grounds that it violates a student's rights will have to look to other statutes, regulations, and standards. A student might argue, for example, that information about an arrest on charges later dismissed is confidential under a state law dealing with arrest records, or that the notation of anonymous, unsubstantiated charges of cheating or stealing violates rights of due process, or that disparaging comments on physical appearance are based on racially discriminatory judgments. In each instance the challenge must be shaped by the nature of the information, the kind of record in which it is contained, and the probable past and future uses of that record in making decisions about the student.

A request to amend a record should be made in writing and addressed to the principal, dean, or other designated administrative official. If the request is denied, or if no answer is given within a reasonable time, or if the institution's informal attempts to reconcile the disagreement seem to be no more than a delaying tactic, a written request for a hearing should be submitted. The "reasonable period" allotted to the institution for its reply to a request for the amendment of a record is not specified in this section of the law, although elsewhere a "reasonable period" is defined as no more than forty-five days. Students and parents should make a note of everything that happens when they ask to have a record corrected: the date of the request, the date of the school's reply, the names of the hearing officers, and the date and nature of the outcome. It may be necessary to use this information in a later enforcement action.

How is a hearing conducted?

Under the FERPA, each educational institution is free to formulate its own procedures for conducting a hearing on a challenge to information in a record, so long as it meets the following requirements:

1. The hearing must be held within a reasonable period after the request is filed.
2. The eligible student or parent must be given reasonable advance notice of the date, time, and place of the hearing. These must be reasonably convenient for the complainant.
3. Although the hearing may be conducted by an official of the institution, the official may not be a person who has "a direct interest in the outcome of the hearing." Of course, it can be argued that any officer of the institution is predisposed to uphold the institution's interests against the individual's challenge. But this provision is designed solely to disqualify a person who would be directly affected by a decision to amend a record, such as the teacher who placed the disputed information in the record or the administrator who will use the information to make a decision about the student.
4. The student or parent must be given a fair opportunity to present arguments and evidence. He may be accompanied, assisted, or represented by a person or persons of his choice: a family member, friend, witness, interpreter, lay advocate (such as a student government representative), or attorney.
5. The hearing decision must be handed down, in writing, within a reasonable time. It must be based solely on evidence presented at the hearing and must contain a summary of the evidence and the reasons for the decision.
6. If the hearing determines that the information is inaccurate, misleading, or a violation of the privacy or other rights of the student, the record must be amended accordingly, and the student or parent must be so informed in writing.[18]

Although the law is not specific on this point, the burden of proof appears to rest upon the student or parent to persuade the institution that the record should be changed.

What happens if the hearing decision denies the request to amend a record?

The school must inform the eligible student or parent that they have the right to insert into the record a statement setting forth the reasons for disagreement with the information. That statement must be maintained as a part of the student's records for as long as the disputed information is itself maintained by the institution, and it must be given to anyone to whom the disputed information is disclosed.[19]

If the student or parent believes that the hearing was not conducted in accordance with the standards required by the FERPA, they may submit a complaint to the Department of Education (see the explanation for complaint procedures later in this chapter).

May school records be disclosed to outsiders?

Under most circumstances, records may not be disclosed without the consent of the student or parent.[20]

The most important disclosures permitted without student or parental consent are these:

1. To personnel within the same school or local school district who have legitimate educational interests in the information.[21] In practice, this may be interpreted to encompass almost anyone employed by the school or school district. The educational institution maintaining the records is responsible for defining which people have a "legitimate educational interest."

2. To officials of another school or district in which the student seeks to enroll or is already enrolled. In such cases, copies of the transferred records and the opportunity for a hearing on the accuracy of their contents must be made available to the eligible student or parent, on request.[22]

3. To certain federal and state educational authorities for purposes of enforcing legal requirements in federally supported education programs. These officials must destroy all personally identifiable data they have gathered when their official duties are completed.[23]

4. To persons involved in granting financial aid for which the student has applied and in enforcing the terms and conditions of aid the student receives.[24]

5. To state and local authorities to whom information is required (not merely permitted) to be disclosed under the provisions of a state statute adopted prior to 19 November 1974.[25] These might include state laws requiring reports of suspected child abuse to a state registry, or reports on juvenile offenders to probation and parole officers, or reports of communicable diseases to local and state boards of health.

6. To testing, research and accrediting organizations, under certain safeguards.[26]

7. Pursuant to a court order or lawfully issued subpoena. The school receiving such an order or subpoena must make a "reasonable effort" to notify the student or parent before it releases the records.[27] Timely notice would allow the person the opportunity to contest the validity of the court order or subpoena on his own behalf.

8. In very narrowly defined emergencies affecting the health and safety of the student or other persons.[28]

In addition, there are circumstances, described in greater detail later in this chapter, in which information may be given to student's parents and in which so-called "directory information" may be released without consent.

It should be remembered that information maintained by campus security officers may be shared with law enforcement officers in the same jurisdiction and that certain kinds of medical and psychiatric records may be shared with persons involved in the student's treatment, as stated earlier.[29]

The FERPA does not require that any of these various categories of records be released without a student's or parent's consent. An educational institution is free to provide consent procedures for these records also. And there are, of course, various state and local laws, regulations, and school board policies more protective than the FERPA, which may ban the release without consent of some kind of information allowed under the FERPA. Where such stronger laws and policies exist, they take precedence over the FERPA.[30]

May students withhold their records from their own parents?

Sometimes. Upon entering college or turning eighteen, a student, known under the FERPA as an "eligible student," assumes control of his or her own FERPA rights and may prevent any other person—including the parents—from obtaining access to most of his or her records without consent. There is, however, a provision in the FERPA allowing a school, at its discretion, to give information to the parents of an eligible student who is a "dependent student" as defined by Section 152 of the Internal Revenue Code of 1954.[31] A dependent student, for tax purposes, is a full-time student whose parents contribute more than half of the student's support even though the student lives away from home and earns some money. The information most frequently given to parents under this provision is the student's grades.

What is "directory information"?

The student's name, address, telephone number, date and place of birth, major field of study, participation in school sports and activities, weight and height (of athletic team members), dates of attendance, degrees and awards, most recent previous school attended, and similar descriptive information.[32]

May directory of information be released without consent?

Yes, unless the eligible student or parent directs otherwise. Each school must compile a list of the categories it intends to classify as directory information. It must give public notice (in the school newspaper, for example) of these categories, inform parents and students of their right to object to the release of information about themselves in any or all of these categories, and allow a sufficient period during which eligible students and parents may exercise that right. The person must inform the school in writing of an objection to the disclosure of particular items about him- or herself or the child. The school is then free to release, without restriction, directory information to which no objection has been submitted.[33]

It is interesting to note that the FERPA extends its most elaborate protection against disclosure without consent to the kinds of personal information least likely to embarrass or cause prejudice against or annoyance to a student.[34] Students are given no similar opportunity to object to the release of other kinds of records that the FERPA permits to be disclosed without consent which often contain far more sensitive personal information.

How is consent to disclosure obtained?

Consent must be written. It must be signed and dated by the eligible student or parent. It must specify what records are to be disclosed, the purpose of the disclosure, and the person or class of persons to whom the records are to be disclosed. The eligible student or parent must be given a copy of any record disclosed with consent upon request.[35]

How can a student or parent find out what records have been disclosed?

Disclosures must be logged. For each disclosure of a record, and for each request for the disclosure of a record, the school must note who made the request, and what were their "legitimate interests" in requesting or obtaining the record. The disclosure log may be inspected by the parent or eligible student. A few requests and disclosures, however, need not be logged: those made to the parent or eligible student himself, those made to personnel within the same school or district who have a "legitimate educational interest" in the record, those made with the consent of the student or parent, and disclosures of directory information.

The disclosure log is considered a part of the student's records and must be maintained as long as the records themselves are maintained. It is important to note that the log must contain all requests for disclosure, whether or not the requests were actually granted.[36]

Once information from a student's records has been disclosed, is there any way of protecting its confidentiality or preventing its redisclosure to others?

Yes, in theory, though not very effectively in practice. When the school discloses information with the student's or parent's consent, the recipient must agree to keep it confidential. If the recipient later wants to redisclose the information, it must obtain the student's or parent's consent. When information is obtained under a circumstance not requiring student or parental consent, it may be redisclosed by the recipient only to another person or agency legally entitled to receive it without student or parental consent. The recipient must log any such redisclosure.[37]

The FERPA's reassurances against redisclosure are rather shaky. Although the institution releasing the record must inform the recipient that redisclosure is forbidden, no written agreement is required, and the ban has little weight unless the recipient is itself an agency or individual subject to some separate legal obligation to maintain confidentiality. Because of this, students and parents should pay close attention to the log of disclosures maintained in the student's records. It should be checked periodically to track disclosures and redisclosures of information. If one cannot actually prevent unauthorized disclosures, it is at least helpful to know what they are.

How is the FERPA enforced?

The Department of Education enforces the act through a special FERPA office in Washington D.C. This office investigates alleged violations of the act and processes complaints. A review board adjudicates cases not resolved by the FERPA Office.[38] The department is also responsible for the regulations that establish standards for the record-keeping procedures of educational institutions subject to the FERPA.[39]

Who may file an enforcement complaint and on what grounds?

Any parent or eligible student may complain to the department of a violation of any provision of the FERPA. Such a violation may concern the student personally: a denial of access to records, a refusal to correct inaccurate information, an unreasonable delay in granting access or correction, a disclosure made without the student's or parent's consent. Or it may concern the record-keeping practices of the institution as they affect the student community as a whole: failure to establish procedures for access to records, to compile lists of records maintained, to provide for hearing, to publish descriptions of directory information, to log disclosures, to protect records from unauthorized disclosure, to give students and parents annual notice of the fact that they have certain rights under the FERPA, or to comply with any other obligation imposed by the statute.

No infraction is too trivial to be reported to the FERPA Office. But one must bear in mind that the complaint procedure is burdensome and protracted, timely relief is unlikely, and the enforcement mechanism is remote from the ordinary student or parent. Complete reliance upon a formal complaint would be unwise; other avenues of redress, such as general student-grievance procedures, pressure by parent associations and student-government associations, publicity, or even professional legal assistance, may be more productive.

How are complaints processed?

Complaints must be submitted in writing to the FERPA Office, at 200 Independence Avenue, S.W., Washington D.C. 20201. No special legal form is required, merely a letter setting out the specifics of the alleged violation. It is helpful to append copies of correspondence with the school regarding the dispute. The FERPA Office will acknowledge receipt of the complaint and will inform the school that a complaint has been filed against it, inviting the school to respond. There will follow a period of investigation and negotiation in which the FERPA Office will determine whether a violation has taken place and, if so, exactly what steps the institution must take to rectify its practices within a specified period of time. The complainant will be notified of the office's findings.[40]

In some instances the FERPA Office may be able to determine immediately whether or not a violation has occurred, and the school may comply without delay. But there is no time limit for investigations, and a complicated complaint could drag out for months, particularly if the school is deliberately obstructive. That is why it is advisable to continue other efforts to resolve a dispute even while a formal complaint is pending.

May the courts intervene to adjudicate FERPA complaints?

Probably yes, although the FERPA itself does not provide for judicial review, and the courts generally have not stepped into this role. The Privacy Protection Study Commission, in its report of July 1977,[41] recommended that the FERPA be amended to permit a parent or eligible student to seek injunctive relief in the courts for any failure by an educational institution to comply with the FERPA. Even if the statute is not amended in this way, redress through the courts is an available, if unused, remedy.

How have the courts interpreted the FERPA?

There has not been much litigation under the FERPA. The most recent case involved a student's mother who sued the Fairfax County (Virginia) School District for informing the community that an "unnamed student" (her daughter) with AIDS would be enrolling in a district school. A federal judge in Virginia dismissed the case, finding that the school's interest in disclosure outweighed the student's privacy interests under the FERPA. An attorney for the child plans to appeal the ruling in the US Court of Appeals for the Fourth Circuit.[42]

In 1987 a federal appeals panel ruled that a noncustodial father had a right to see his child's report card and the FERPA gave him the right to sue in court to enforce that right.[43] In 1980 a New York State court held that the FERPA did not require a university to release transcripts to a student who failed to pay tuition.[44] And finally, a US court in New York held that FERPA-protected documents could not be disclosed automatically upon discovery without first weighing the privacy interests.[45]

What can the Department of Education do if a school does not comply with a decision by the FERPA Office?

Proceedings may be instituted by a special review board to withdraw all federal funds given to the institution through the US Office of Education.[46] The nature of this ultimate sanction for a violation of the FERPA helps explain why students and parents frequently have difficulty exercising their statutory rights with respect to school records. The sanction is wholly disproportionate to the seriousness of most violations, and is therefore most unlikely to be invoked. No one really expects that all federal funding will be withdrawn from a public high school just because it has refused to let a few students examine some of their records. In fact, the withdrawal of funds could harm the students much more than even a major violation of the FERPA. Also the tortuous proceedings required in order to terminate funding completely foreclose any hope of timely relief for the individual whose FERPA rights have been violated. So far, no institution has suffered this final sanction.

What other laws, in addition to the FERPA, protect the privacy of students?

A few states have statutes that expand or clarify the rights of access and confidentiality provided by the FERPA.[47] The federal statute established minimum standards for the maintenance and dissemination of student records, and any further protection available under state legislation takes precedence. Such state statutes may apply to certain schools not subject to the FERPA or may prohibit the dissemination of some kinds of information from student records that the FERPA permits. State freedom of information laws and privacy (fair information practices) laws contain provisions applicable to the records of students, particularly those personally identifiable records maintained by state and local agencies other than schools. There are many government agencies that collect information about students: public health departments, child abuse registries, welfare departments, hospitals, mental health clinics, police, juvenile courts, parole and probation agencies, social services agencies, and many more. The laws pertaining to some of these are described in other chapters of this book.

A few states have statutes protecting the confidentiality of communications between students and school counselors.[48] In other states the content of such communications is not legally privileged, although any records maintained by counselors are of course covered by the FERPA and applicable state laws.

NOTES

1. 20 U.S.C. § 1232g., as amended by Pub. L. No. 96-46 4LL(c).
2. 45 C.F.R. § 99.1.
3. 20 U.S.C. § 1232g. (a); 45 C.F.R. § 99.3.

4. 20 U.S.C. § 1232g. (e); 45 C.F.R. § 99.5.
5. 20 U.S.C. § 1232g. (a)(4); 45 C.F.R. § 99.3.
6. *Id.*
7. 20 U.S.C. § 1232g(a)(1)(B) and (C); 45 C.F.R. §§ 99.7 and 99.12.
8. 20 U.S.C. § 1232g(a)(1)(B) and (C); 45 C.F.R. §§ 99.7 and 99.12.
9. 20 U.S.C. § 1232g(e); 45 C.F.R. §§ 99.6.
10. 20 U.S.C. § 1232g(a)(1)(A).
11. 45 C.F.R. § 99.11.
12. 45 C.F.R. § 99.8.
13. 45 C.F.R. § 99.11.
14. 45 C.F.R. § 99.8.
15. 45 C.F.R. § 99.5.
16. 20 U.S.C. § 1232g(a)(2); 45 C.F.R. § 99.20.
17. Cong. Rec. S21.488 Dec. 13, 1974.
18. 20 U.S.C. § 1232g(a)(2); 45 C.F.R. §§ 99.21 and 99.22.
19. *Id.*
20. 20 U.S.C. § 1232g(b).
21. 45 C.F.R. § 99.31.
22. 45 C.F.R. §§ 99.31 and 99.34.
23. 45 C.F.R. §§ 99.31 and 99.35.
24. 45 C.F.R. § 99.31.
25. *Id.*
26. *Id.*
27. *Id.*
28. 45 C.F.R. §§ 99.31 and 99.36.
29. 45 C.F.R. § 99.3.
30. 20 U.S.C. § 1232g(b)(1).
31. 45 C.F.R. § 99.31.
32. 20 U.S.C. § 1232g(a)(5)(A); 45 C.F.R. § 99.3.
33. 20 U.S.C. § 1232g(a)(5)(A); and (B); 45 C.F.R. § 99.37.
34. Privacy Protection Study Commission, *Personal Privacy in an Information Society*, 427 (US Government Printing Office, July 1977).
35. 20 U.S.C. § 1232g (1) and (b) (2)(A); 45 C.F.R. § 99.30.
36. 20 U.S.C. § 1232g (b)(4)(A); 45 C.F.R. § 99.32.
37. 20 U.S.C. § 1232g(b)(4).(B).
38. 20 U.S.C. § 1232g(g).
39. 45 C.F.R. § 99.
40. 45 C.F.R. § 99.63.
41. Privacy Protection Study Commission, *supra* note 34, at 438. *See,* however, *Girardier v. Webster College*, 563 F.2d. 1267 (11th. Cir. 1977).
42. *Child v. Robert R. Spillane, et al.* USDC-E.D.Va (1989).

43. *Fay v. South Colonie Central School District* 802 F.2d 21 (2d Cir. 1986).
44. *Spas v. Wharton, et al.* 431 N.Y.S. 2d 638 (1980).
45. *Rios v. Read* 73 F.R.D. 589 (E.D.N.Y. 1977).
46. 20 U.S.C. § 1232g(f); 45 C.F.R. § 99.64–67.
47. *See, e.g.*, Cal. Educ. Code §§ 967, 10931, 22509, and 25430; Conn. Gen. Stat. Ann. § 10-156; Del. Code Ann. tit. 41, § 4114; Ill., Rev. Stat. ch. 112, para. 50–1 *et. seq.*; Mass. Ann. Laws ch. 71, § 340; Miss. Code Ann. §§ 317-15-1; Neb. Rev. Stat. §§ 79-4, 156 and 157; Wis. Stat. Ann. § 118.125.
48. See Conn. Gen. Stat. Ann. § 10-154; Idaho Code § 9-203; Ky. Rev. Stat. § 421-216; Me. Rev. Stat. Ann. tit. 20, § 806; Mont. Rev. Codes Ann. § 93-701 *et seq.*; Nev. Rev. Stat. § 49.290 *et seq.*; N.C. Gen Stat. § 5-43.4; N.D. Cent. Code § 81-06-06.1; S.D. Compiled Laws Ann. § 19-2-5.1 and 5.2.

PART 2

Personal Information and the Private Sector

IX

Employment Records, Monitoring, and Testing

The workplace is where most adults spend roughly half of their waking hours. It is not surprising, therefore, that employment practices affect a broad range of privacy rights. With the exception of polygraph testing, there are few areas of workplace activities that are covered by the U.S. Constitution or national privacy laws. Accordingly, employers have a great deal of leeway in collecting data on their employees, regulating access to personnel files, and disclosing file contents to outsiders. In addition to the issue of personnel files, workplace privacy involves such practices as polygraph testing, drug testing, computer and telephone monitoring, and interference with personal lifestyle. All of these practices stem from a combination of modern employer concerns—employee theft, drug abuse, productivity, courtesy and the protection of trade secrets—and technological advances that make it more economical to engage in monitoring and testing. The result for employees, however, is a dramatic increase in workplace surveillance. Unprecedented numbers of workers are urinating into bottles for employer-run, drug-testing programs. Phone operators for most telephone companies, airlines, and other service industries never know when a supervisor will be listening in. Thousands of data entry operators have their every keystroke recorded by the very computers on which they are working. Surveillance is so thorough in some offices that employers can check to see exactly when employees leave their work stations to go to the bathroom and how long they take. Polygraph tests caused well-documented misery and abuse for American workers for decades, and only in 1988 did Congress bar the use of lie detectors in most private sector workplaces.

Despite the general absence of federal protection for worker privacy, there are some important limits on employers, due mainly to a variety of state constitutional provisions and statutes and the emergence of a "common law" right to privacy that creative attorneys are invoking on behalf of employees who have been victimized by intrusive practices. In fact a study by the

Bureau of National Affairs showed that the nationwide average jury verdict during the 1985 through 1987 period in workplace privacy cases brought by employees against their employers was $316,000, while the national average from 1979 through 1980 was zero. In addition, the study showed that the total number of workplace privacy verdicts against employers nationwide increased twentyfold between the 1981 through 1984 period and the 1985 through 1987 period.[1]

PERSONNEL FILES: COLLECTION, ACCESS, AND DISCLOSURE OF DATA ON EMPLOYEES

How do employers get information about their employees and about their job applicants?

Often from the employee or applicant himself, through questionnaires, interviews, and responses to an employer's periodic queries during the person's period of employment. In addition, personality and psychological tests, polygraph tests (illegal as of 1989 in most workplaces), skills tests, and medical examinations may be performed, both before and during employment.

In considering job applicants, employers may also question former employers and professional references, ask for educational, military, credit, and medical records, and check with the police and FBI for arrest and conviction information. Some employers make these background checks themselves; others use a credit-reporting agency to do the job for them. A credit-reporting agency may also be asked to conduct an investigation on an employee who is being considered for a promotion. For certain kinds of employment requiring security clearance, a government agency will run a thorough security investigation involving a search of FBI, police, and other government databases and at times interviews with colleagues, neighbors, and acquaintances.

While a person is employed, the employer may receive information about him from outside sources. Medical information submitted on claims under company insurance plans is usually available to at least some management personnel. Employers may be contacted by third parties with regard to a person's loan or mortgage applications, debts, suits, or garnishments. Law-enforcement and other government agencies may inform employers about the nature of their dealings with a particular employee.

Some believe that employers increasingly are turning to public record checks to verify applicants' backgrounds. One consultant, Richard C. Long, attributes this to past employers' unwillingness to give candid references due to a sharp increase in defamation lawsuits and to applicants' exaggerating their credentials. Long adds that there is a trend towards holding employers liable when an employee whose background shows a clear history of a certain type of criminal history commits a crime of that nature during the course of employment. Long's company, National Employment Screening Service, conducts records checks for a fee.[2]

Are there restrictions on the kinds of information that employers may obtain?

As a practical matter, very few. There are some state laws that forbid employers to ask applicants for certain kinds of information. For example, Illinois, California, Massachusetts, and New York prohibit most employers from asking applicants about arrests not followed by a conviction. Massachusetts bars inquiries about treatment or institutionalization in a mental hospital; Michigan forbids employers to keep records describing an employee's political associations or nonemployment activities; Maryland law forbids employers to ask about psychiatric or psychological problems unless these have a direct bearing on the applicant's fitness for the particular job in question.[3] But with a handful of exceptions such as these, employers are legally free to ask applicants just about anything, including the most intimate details of their personal lives. Employers are forbidden by state and federal laws to discriminate against applicants on the basis of certain factors—race, sex, age, handicap, religion, national origin—but they are not forbidden to ask the questions. (Indeed, maintaining records on these factors of both successful and unsuccessful applicants may be required in order to measure an employer's compliance with antidiscrimination laws.) Under most circumstances they may even ask applicants to reveal information that is legally confidential; a frequent item on application forms is a question about juvenile offenses, even though the records of juvenile convictions are statutorily protected and may be sealed or expunged after a person reaches majority.

If there is doubt about an employer's right to ask for certain types of information, applicants are routinely requested to sign waivers of confidentiality that permit the employer (or a credit-reporting agency working for it) to obtain information and records from virtually any source. Unless the applicant is in a strong bargaining position—which of course most applicants are not—he has no realistic choice but to sign the waiver. At most, it may be possible for an applicant to ask that the employer make a vaguely worded waiver more specific, for example, by indicating which sources and record-keepers he intends to query and by inserting an expiration date.

Tipping the balance even further against the applicant's privacy are the various state and federal laws that either permit or require certain kinds of information for employment and occupational-licensing purposes. The most common focus of such laws is arrest information, even where an arrest was not followed by conviction and bears no rational relationship to the nature of the employment.

Applicants who may be tempted to protect themselves against an embarrassing or damaging disclosure by lying must remember that the disclosure may occur anyway in the course of the employer's background check or an investigation by a credit-reporting agency. Some employers view the deliberate submission of misinformation on an application as sufficient reason for refusal to hire or for firing an employee already on the job.

Are employment records confidential under law?

If the employer is a federal agency, the Privacy Act of 1974 defines the confidentiality of employment records. The act permits disclosures of federal-agency employee records without the employee's consent only for "routine uses," in response to the written request of a law enforcement agency, or in compliance with a court order. In states with analogous privacy acts, employment records held by state and local agencies may enjoy similar protection. A few states have special statutes protecting the confidentiality of state employees' records.[4] Occasionally, union contracts provide some protection. Otherwise the matter lies solely at the discretion of the employer. To understand just how crucial the exercise of that discretion really is, one must recall that employment files ordinarily contain much more than strictly job-related information; they may have medical, family, sexual, financial, political, and other personal data, and possibly the subjective comments of colleagues and supervisors. The confidentiality of all this information lies completely at the employer's mercy.[5]

Does this mean there is no legal recourse for a person whose employer has divulged information about him without his permission?

Not entirely. In some very special circumstances there may be redress. If the information is false and defamatory and if it is directly responsible for causing a serious tangible injury to the employee, there may be grounds for recovery of damages in a defamation lawsuit.

Employers routinely disclose information about their employees to other employers, unions, law-enforcement agencies and various other government agencies, banks and creditors, insurance companies, and private individuals. Some of these disclosures may be legally mandated or in compliance with the employee's own wishes; others may be offensive to his sense of privacy or may even cause him actual harm. Although most of the information disclosed by employers is job-related, some disclosures may reveal aspects of the employee's personal life, such as sexual orientation, political associations, or family problems. Yet unless the circumstances are unusual, the private employer cannot be legally penalized for violating the employee's privacy.

Where the employer is a government agency subject to the federal Privacy Act or similar state law, an aggrieved employee can bring a lawsuit for illegal disclosures. Under the Privacy Act, for example, a person who suffers an "adverse effect" because of a "willful and intentional" disclosure of records made in violation of the act can sue for damages of at least $1,000, and an official who "knowingly and willfully" makes such a disclosure can be fined up to $5,000.[6] But for most private employees, there is no legally established "expectation of confidentiality" regarding their employment records. Unless a disclosure rises to the level of an actual defamation (a matter on which an attorney's advice should be sought), there is no readily available remedy, however offensive or prejudicial the disclosure may be.

Is there a legal recourse for a person whose former employer gives a damaging reference to a prospective employer?

Not much, unless the reference actually contains false and defamatory statements. People sometimes attribute their inability to obtain employment to damaging statements made by a former employer. Assuming that a person is able to get access to the references in employment files, a lawsuit for defamation may be possible. Oral statements present a greater problem since there is unlikely to be any documentary evidence or third-party witness. The situation is more favorable when the reference is delivered to the prospective employer by a credit-reporting agency, for here the person is entitled, under the Fair Credit Reporting Act, to hear at least the "nature and substance" of the information in the agency's files.

Having discovered the nature of the former employer's reference and having determined, on an attorney's advice, that a defamation suit is not a practical option, the employee can only attempt to combat the effects of the derogatory reference by giving his own explanation and interpretation to prospective employers and perhaps by presenting testimonials from other employers, supervisors, and coworkers.

If the advantages seem to be stacked heavily in the employer's favor, it should be noted that employers seem to be increasingly deterred by the threat of defamation suits — which are a nuisance and an expense to defend even if the plaintiff eventually loses — and therefore increasingly loath to give wholly unflattering references. In fact, employers sometimes claim that they hesitate to give even clearly truthful derogatory references for fear of lawsuits. While that claim is probably overstated, more and more employers are taking steps to make provisions for employees to examine—and in some cases comment upon and rebut—the performance evaluations that go into their files and that could be disclosed in references to future employers.

At times, employers must investigate job applicant's backgrounds to avoid subsequent charges of "negligent hiring." For instance, the Minnesota Supreme Court imposed liability to the owner of an apartment complex for hiring an apartment manager who later raped a tenant. The owner had not investigated the employee's prior criminal record.[7]

Although some states have enacted laws restricting employers' inquiries into certain areas such as arrest records, private employers generally may require disclosure of a broad range of data from job applicants that in the public sector are protected by a right to privacy. Most states adhere to the idea that job applicants have the choice of whether they want to answer personal questions. However, no court has held that employers can be liable for rejecting job applicants who refuse to answer nondiscriminatory questions.[8]

Do employees of government agencies have a right of access to employment records?

Most employees of government agencies have a right of access, under statute or regulation, to at least some of their employment records. Employees and former employees of federal agencies have a right of access, as well as a right of correction, under the Privacy Act of 1974. In fact, federal employees are the primary users of the act's access provisions. Most states have analogous privacy or open records acts, and so state and local government employees usually have access and correction rights. Access provisions commonly are contained in the state civil service regulations. All of these laws and regulations differ in their designations of certain kinds of records that employees may not see; frequent exceptions are medical records, performance evaluations, test results and security and investigatory files.

Do private sector employees have a right of access to their own employment records?

Sometimes. There is no national law guaranteeing workers'

rights to see files about them held by employers. At last count, 12 states—California, Connecticut, Maine, Massachusetts, Michigan, New Hampshire, Ohio (employer-held medical files), Oregon, Pennsylvania, Vermont, Virginia, and Wisconsin—had statutes granting employees the right to see, copy, and correct their personnel records.[9]

In the late 1970s, several major corporations, seeking to show Congress that federal legislation was not warranted, adopted "in-house privacy policies" granting employees access to their records, as well as the right to correct inaccurate data and limit disclosures to outsiders. No one ever determined precisely how many US companies adopted such programs, but IBM, the first corporation to do so (in the mid-1970s), in 1983 said it had received 2,397 requests for copies of its policy.[10]

Seeing one's own personnel file usually is a routine matter. An employee merely needs to ask his supervisor or personnel department and, in more cases than not, the file is provided. However, there are still significant numbers of employees who are denied access to their own records. A 1989 survey of 126 corporations employing nearly four million people showed that 87 percent granted workers access to their files. While this is up from 77 percent in 1979, it still means that employers of some 500,000 workers do not permit them to see their own files.[11] The percentages probably are worse for the entire workforce because the survey covered Fortune 500 companies—those most likely to have formal policies. One example of an employee not having routine access to his file was the case of Paul Sherbo, formerly a reporter with the *Colorado Springs Sun.* Upon leaving his job in 1983, Sherbo asked for a copy of his personnel file. First the company told him that he could not see it. Then it said he could see it but not copy it. The newspaper's personnel director told Sherbo's attorney that if Sherbo was given his file, they would have to let all employees obtain their records. "We really don't want to get in a situation where all our employees come in and say 'I want my file, I want my file.' I see no reason to do this. I'm curious as to why he [Sherbo] wants it," said John Harrington, the personnel director. Sherbo said when he left the Navy, it gave him copies of all his records—service, pay, medical and dental. "I realized after that it was good to have your files."[12] Sherbo later obtained his file from the newspaper.

Other cases show that in-house privacy policies are at times not worth much. One IBM saleswoman who sued the company said after twelve years with the company, "I never saw my personnel file while I was there, and I don't remember anyone encouraging us to look at it. It definitely wasn't well-communicated to us because I would have wanted to see my file," she said. Her attorney was able to obtain the file through court discovery.[13] Another example of a "forgotten" in-house policy came in late 1981 when the Equitable Life Assurance Society was trying to stave off a union organizing campaign by data entry clerks in its Syracuse office. A major source of dispute was Equitable's policy of monitoring clerks' "keystrokes," that is, every time their fingers entered data into the machines. The company said it would gauge performance evaluations by the monitoring reports. But when clerks sought access to records showing their output, the company denied the requests.[14] In 1980 hearings held by the US Labor Department, an Equitable vice president described the company's employee privacy policy as an effort to create a better working environment, adding, "We [must] remain sensitive to both the individual needs of our workers and to the values of our society."[15] In 1984, Equitable recognized the union. The two sides agreed to a contract that gave clerks access to all records relating to pay but which did not end computer monitoring.

Do employees of private companies have the right to correct or amend their records?

Not under federal or state statutes. Even the twelve state employee access laws do not specify a right to correct records. The above mentioned in-house privacy policies nearly always included a right to correct records, and it should be noted there are few incentives for employers to maintain inaccurate data in personnel files.

What kind of redress does the common law offer?

Under the common law—a branch of tort law dealing with civil wrongs—privacy can be divided into four areas: (1)

appropriation of the name and likeness of another; (2) unreasonable intrusion upon the seclusion of another; (3) unreasonable publicity given to another person's private life; and (4) publicity that unreasonably places a person in a false light before the public.[16] In rare cases in which these elements combine, employees can win damages against their employers. In 1985 a United Airlines flight attendant sought a waiver from the airline's medical examiner of the weight limit imposed by the airline for appearance purposes. Her private physician gave the airline's medical examiner confidential medical data on the employee's gynecological and other physical problems and on her contraceptive methods. The medical examiner disclosed much of this data to the attendant's male supervisor and made other comments about it in the presence of another supervisor. A jury found that these disclosures were an invasion of the flight attendant's privacy and granted her $14,000 in compensatory damages. Another $20,000 in punitive damages was reversed on appeal.[17]

In another case, an IBM employee followed his supervisor's advice and met several times with a physician under company contract. Under IBM's in-house privacy policy, supervisors were not allowed to have direct contact with local physicians connected with an Employee Assistance Program. But the physician called the supervisor, informed her that the employee was "paranoid," and recommended immediate psychiatric treatment. This and subsequent communications from the psychiatrist were disclosed to several other managers and supervisors at IBM. The employee sued for breach of privacy under the Massachusetts constitution. A federal appeals court, while holding that it was not an unreasonable intrusion upon the employee's privacy merely to inform certain managers that he had taken advantage of a company program to obtain unspecified medical treatment, found that disclosure of the employee's visit to a psychiatrist *could* be an invasion of privacy because of the paramount importance of confidentiality in the physician-patient relationship. Accordingly, the appeals court ruled the employee had a right to a jury trial on his allegations that IBM breached his privacy.[18]

The Oklahoma Supreme Court came to a different conclusion in a similar case. A Texaco supervisor referred an em-

ployee to a company physician who, in turn, referred him to a
psychiatrist. The supervisor found out and allegedly disclosed the fact to several coworkers. The state high court
ruled that no invasion of the employee's privacy had occurred
because the data in the employee's medical records were of
legitimate concern to his supervisor. The court also found that
no unreasonable publicity of the employee's private life exis-
ted because only a limited number of coworkers knew of his
psychiatric treatment.[19]

Employees increasingly are taking their employers to
courts for defamation, which involves injury to someone due
to the disclosure of false data.[20] But companies are free to give
accurate job references. In 1984 a Chesapeake and Potomac
Telephone Company (C&P) employee applied for a position
with several other Bell companies in other regions. C&P
informed its counterparts the employee had taken ninety
days' sick leave, when in fact she had taken seventy days. The
allowable number was twelve days. The employee sued C&P
for giving out bad and inaccurate job references, but a federal
judge — in dismissing the suit — said the references were close
enough to the truth to stand up in court.[21]

What other kinds of disclosures have led to court dis-
putes?

A leading case is the Supreme Court's 1979 decision in
Detroit Edison v. NLRB,[22] in which the court upheld the
authority of employers to promise employees that certain
sensitive types of data will not be disclosed without their
consent. In subsequent cases, however, corporate interpretations of what constitutes confidential employee data have not
always held up. The National Institute of Occupational Safety
and Health (NIOSH), seeking to survey health hazards at
a Westinghouse plant, subpoenaed its employee medical records. Westinghouse insisted it would not respond until the
employees authorized release of their confidential medical
files and NIOSH promised not to share them with anyone
else. The court held that the strong public interest in facilitat-
ing research and investigations by NIOSH justified "the
minimal intrusion into the privacy which surrounds the
employee's medical records." Acknowledging the sensitivity

of the medical files, the court said NIOSH was required to give prior notice to affected employees and allow them to assert their own personal privacy claims.[23]

Employers also have been required to turn over personnel files to administrative agencies, such as federal and state equal employment opportunity commissions investigating allegations of discrimination. Human rights commissions and the EEOC routinely reject employer claims of confidentiality.[24]

In two instances, the National Labor Relations Board overruled company policies in the face of union demands for employee records. One time, New Jersey Bell refused to give to the Communications Workers Union three personnel files of employees who had been disciplined for being late to a mandatory overtime meeting. Citing its in-house policy, New Jersey Bell asked the union to get signed consents from the employees. The union ordered employees not to consent, and the company refused to release the files. The NLRB ruled that the union's need for relevant records under federal labor law outweighed a voluntary company policy.[25] Similarly, the board ordered a Utah company to give records on two employees who were disciplined differently for the same offense to the International Brotherhood of Electrical Workers, even though the union ignored the company's written policy and demanded the records without the employees' written consent.[26]

Are there guidelines describing improved policies in the areas of access to, correction of, and disclosure of personnel records?

Yes. The Privacy Protection Study Commission, in guidelines issued in 1977, tried to balance the concerns of employers and employees in three areas: access to records, correction of records, and internal disclosures of information. These guidelines can be summarized as follows:

1. *Access to Records.* While finding that fairness demands that job applicants and employees be allowed to see and copy records an employer maintains about them, the commission recognized employers' general reluctance to allow access to test scores, records requiring professional inter-

pretation, and information supplied by confidential services such as references. As a result, the panel recommended that:

- Employers designate clearly what records applicants, employees, or former employees will be allowed to inspect;
- Access be permitted to evaluations of employee's performance or potential that can be used for promotion and placement and that access need not be given to records indicating a high potential for advancement;
- Access be permitted to any records of security investigations that are placed in a personnel file;
- Employees be allowed to examine, copy, correct, amend, or dispute the contents of credit reports used by an employer, although the Fair Credit Reporting Act requires only that employers notify individuals when such reports are used;
- Access to information in medical records be permitted when the employer provides medical care; in other situations access should be given to the employee directly or indirectly through a medical professional; and
- Access be given to insurance records maintained on employees, former employees, or dependents in an employer's capacity as an insurance plan administrator.

2. *Correction of Records.* The commission found that confidentiality could not be separated from accuracy, recommending that employees who question the accuracy, timeliness, or thoroughness of records be able to correct and amend those records; where a correction is made, the employer should include the correction or amendment in any subsequent disclosure; and when an employer rejects the requested correction or amendment, fairness demands that the employee's statement of the dispute be incorporated into the record and forwarded when the records are disclosed.

3. *Internal Disclosure of Documents.* The panel concluded that employers have a duty to see that information generated as one part of the employer-employee relationship not be disclosed to others in the organization in ways that are unfair to the employee. The commission recommended that:

- Personnel and payroll records be available internally only to authorized users on a need-to-know basis;
- Security records or records relating to security investigations be maintained apart from other records, but that no access need be given to the employees unless the information is incorporated into their personnel files or is used for discipline, termination, promotion, or evaluation;
- Medical records used for work restrictions be kept confidential and that no diagnostic or treatment information be made available for use in any employment decision;
- Where an employer offers voluntary medical services, those medical records be segregated from other records, and not used in employment-related decisions without the employee's consent;
- Identifiable life or health insurance records be separately maintained and not made available for use in employment decisions; and that
- Records of work related insurance (compensation, disability, sick pay) be available internally only to authorized recipients on a need-to-know basis.[27]

What is the extent of employee monitoring in the United States?

As of 1987, nearly seven million American office workers were subject to some form of computer monitoring, and the number is likely to grow considerably throughout the 1990s, according to a study by the congressional Office of Technology Assessment (OTA).[28] US firms involved in computer monitoring include American Express, AT&T, and information-in-tensive industries like banking, insurance, and credit. Monitoring of workers in the United States usually involves recording individual computer operator keystrokes—ostensibly designed to increase productivity—or listening in on telephone operators—supposedly to promote courtesy and efficiency. European workers enjoy stronger privacy protection than their American counterparts. For example, Sweden and West Germany have required employers to study group rates rather than individual ones. And Italian workers affiliated with the

Federation of Metal Workers were able to use existing law to win an agreement with IBM of Italy to prohibit individual work monitoring.[29]

A survey by Columbia University Professor Alan F. Westin revealed that twenty major US unions had adopted policies against monitoring, while only one-third of corporations surveyed had adopted "fair work evaluation policies."[30] The OTA study found that "[i]n nearly all case examples, employees had little input concerning the monitoring system, and in only a few cases was it clear that they had access to information about their own performance or the ability to contest wrong information. In nearly all these cases, the workers . . . considered the monitoring system unfair." Further, the OTA concluded: "The reasons why concerns about autonomy, dignity and privacy are praised in electronic monitoring have to do with the fact that computers are ever-vigilant; unlike human supervisors, they do not tire of observing and recording the minutiae of employee performance."[31] However, the OTA found there were no federal laws to address computer monitoring, despite the fact that the practice implicated employee privacy rights, caused stress, and proved to be counterproductive in many instances. The Equitable Life Assurance Society's use of computer monitoring was a case in point. Without notice or discussion, the company's Syracuse office in the early 1980s installed a system capable of monitoring each keystroke entered by its computer operators. The workers resisted. They were organized by 9 to 5, the National Association of Working Women, an affiliate of the Service Employees International Union (SEIU). The union demanded a halt to monitoring and the maintenance of secret files on employees. At first Equitable refused to recognize the union, but in November 1984 it agreed to do so. Although it continued its computer monitoring program, the company agreed to let employees see their performance records.[32]

What about telephone monitoring?

Phone monitoring has long been practiced by companies with operators that deal regularly with the public, including AT&T, airlines, hotels, insurance firms, retail stores, and mail-order houses. In 1987, Representative Don Edwards (D-CA) introduced legislation to require an audible "beep tone" to indicate the monitoring of a call, but the bill—adamantly opposed by phone companies, airlines, and other service industries that regularly monitor their employees' phones—never made it out of committee.

New technologies have increased management's power to listen in selectively. The Integrated Service Digital Network (ISDN), a system first used by federal agencies, can be programmed to listen in on employees and pick up key phrases from their telephone conversations. "Depending upon the motives of management, technology like ISDN could be used to detect a worker's religious or political involvement, union activity or personal problems," stated the union, 9 to 5, National Association of Working Women.[33] The union said Ohio Bell announced that it changed headsets to enable the company to gather more data on employees' "work product." But the new devices also permitted managers to listen to private conversations between coworkers and thus acquire greater data on workers.[34]

In 1983 the US Court of Appeals for the Eleventh Circuit ruled that a company violated federal wiretap laws when it monitored a conversation in which an employee told a friend she hoped to get another job. Noting the company's policy against monitoring personal phone calls, the court rejected the company's position that a "business exception" permitted such monitoring.[35] But the same court upheld a business that eavesdropped on—and caught—an employee it suspected of divulging trade secrets to a competitor.[36]

Finally it is important to note that the Communications Workers of America have testified before Congress that in West Virginia and Wisconsin, where state laws bar phone monitoring, there has been no decline in service quality or productivity.[37]

Can employees be disciplined or fired for their off-the-job activity?

Probably. There are no statutes covering off-duty behavior for private sector employees, though a few local ordinances bar discrimination based on sexual preference, and one case does suggest there are limits. The main court case was *Rulon-*

Miller v. IBM, in which an IBM saleswoman was awarded $300,000 in damages by a California jury after she was fired for dating a competitor's salesman. The plaintiff had an outstanding employee performance record. But she refused to stop dating her boyfriend, despite threats of dismissal from her superiors. IBM fired her, and she filed suit, charging breach of contract and intentional infliction of emotional distress. Rulon-Miller prevailed after her attorney read to the jury an IBM chairman's statement that an employee's private life was none of IBM's business as long as it did not affect the company.[38]

Is drug testing a way of regulating off-duty performance?

Yes, but that has not deterred many corporations. A 1988 Gallup survey showed that 28 percent of the largest US corporations—including AT&T and General Motors—are using drug tests to screen job applicants, and the number is expected to grow sharply through the early 1990s. The survey also showed that half of the firms engaged in drug testing started in 1987 or 1988.

Connecticut, Kansas, Iowa, Minnesota, Rhode Island, Montana, and Vermont have enacted laws that restrict random drug testing of most workers—except those applying for "safety-sensitive jobs." Maryland and Nebraska statutes set procedures and standards for drug testing. Several of these laws bar dismissal of those workers who complete successful rehabilitation programs, but Utah and Louisiana have given employers broad authority for random drug testing.

Have there been successful court challenges to drug testing by private employers?

Yes. On 30 October 1987 a San Francisco jury awarded $485,000 to a railroad employee who refused to take a drug test on the ground that it violated her right to privacy under the California Constitution. The jury said that the Southern Pacific Company violated the employee's privacy and also breached its duty of good faith and fair dealing and intentionally inflicted emotional distress.[39]

In June 1988, Alameda County Superior Court Judge

Michael E. Ballachey became the first to bar a private employer from conducting pre-employment drug testing under the California Constitution. Judge Ballachey issued a preliminary junction against publisher Matthew Bender, Inc., which is owned by the Times Mirror Company. The company said it would appeal.[40]

On the other hand, the US Supreme Court, by a 7 to 2 vote in March 1989, upheld the constitutionality of Federal Railroad Administration (FRA) rules that called for drug testing of train crew members after an accident. The Court found that the government's interest in prompting public safety was "compelling" and that rules were sufficiently targeted to crews involved in accidents to minimize intrusions on privacy. In dissent, Justice Thurgood Marshall accused the Court of sacrificing fundamental freedoms in the name of exigency, as it did in the Japanese-American relocation camp case during World War II and a McCarthy-era internal subversion case in the 1950s.[41]

What about drug testing of government employees?

The Supreme Court in March 1989 also ruled 5 to 4 that the Customs Service drug testing program did not violate the Fourth Amendment's prohibitions against unreasonable searches and seizure. The Court reasoned that the Customs Service's interest in preserving the integrity of armed agents and those involved in drug interdiction outweighed privacy concerns. However, the majority decision did not give a legal "blank check" to drug testing of all federal employees. In fact, it said the Customs Service had failed to justify drug testing of employees with access to classified data. The decision's impact is further clouded by the fact that four justices dissented, including conservative Antonin Scalia, who said that the Customs Service had not even demonstrated there was a drug problem or that urinalysis testing would improve matters. He called the program "a kind of immolation of privacy and human dignity in symbolic opposition to drug use," adding that "symbolism, even symbolism for so worthy a cause as the abolition of unlawful drugs, cannot validate an otherwise unreasonable search."[42] As of April 1989, there were some forty challenges to federal drug testing programs pending in the courts. These programs potentially affect millions of employees since they are expected to set an example for the private sector as well.

Are polygraphs still used in the private sector?

Yes, but their use should be sharply curtailed by a federal law signed into effect 27 June 1988. The law is the result of a twenty-year legislative effort begun by Senator Sam Ervin. The law, known as the "Polygraph Protection Act," bars the use of polygraphs for nearly all types of pre-employment screening by private employers, except for personnel in security positions or those handling controlled substances. It also establishes guidelines for polygraph use in internal company investigations.

Why did Congress restrict the use of so-called "lie detectors"?

First, polygraphs do not detect lies. The machines measure respiration and pulse and are premised upon the assumption that physiological reactions determine that a person is lying. Modern science has debunked these myths. Studies revealed that the polygraph's chances for accuracy in an open-ended interview were not much better than 50 percent. Furthermore, it seems many employers who used polygraphs were not interested in accuracy as much as in intimidating their employees into confessing intimate details about their lives. As President Nixon once put it, "I don't know how accurate polygraphs are, but I know they scare the hell out of people!"

Second, polygraphs produced a long history of abuse of employee rights. The Coors Beer Company polygrapher used to ask job applicants about their sexual habits, whether they stole from their mother, or whether they had ever committed an undetected crime. Women often ended up in situations in which they were sexually harassed by polygraph examiners. Some employees over the years have successfully sued employers for the most abusive practices, winning jury awards ranging from $200,000 to $5 million.

The prohibition on polygraph use was long overdue. But weeks after the law was enacted, Northwestern University

Professor Joel Rosenfeld announced he was working on a different kind of polygraph—a "mind lie detector." The machine monitors brain waves, and is based on the premise that brain waves change when one is lying. Professor Rosenfeld predicts his "mind detector" will be available by 1990. A Congressional staffer said the new polygraph law bars such devices in the employment setting as well.[43]

NOTES

1. Ira Michael Shephard and Robert L. Duston, *Workplace Privacy* (Bureau of National Affairs, 1987) pp. 1–2; herein cited as "BNA Study."
2. *Privacy Times*, Nov. 8, 1988.
3. *See, e.g., Federal Personal Data Systems Subject to the Privacy Act of 1974, Second Annual Report of the President*, Calendar Year 1976 (Government Printing Office, 1977) and subsequent Annual Reports.
4. *See, e.g.,* Colo. Rev. Stat., § 24-50-127.
5. There are minor exceptions to this generalization; for example, the Michigan Employee Right-to-Know Act places some restrictions on the kinds of information, particularly adverse information, that an employer may disclose.
6. U.S.C. § 552a(g) and (i).
7. *Ponticas v. K.M.S. Investments*, 331 N.W.2d 907 (Minn. 1983).
8. BNA Study, 47.
9. Cal. Lab Code 1198.5 (West 1987); Conn. Gen. Stat. Ann. § 31-128b (West 1987); Me. Rev. Stat. Ann. tit. 26, § 631 (1986); Mass. Gen. Laws Ann. ch. 149, § 52C (West 1987); Mich. Stat. Ann. § 1762(1)–(5) (Callaghan 1982); N.H. Rev. Stat. Ann. § 275.56 (1986); Ohio Rev. Code Ann. § 4133.23(A) (Anderson 1973); Or. Rev. Stat. § 652.750(2) (1981); Pa. Stat. Ann. tit. 43, § 1322 (Purdon 1986); Vt. Stat. Ann. tit. 1 § 317(b)(7)(1985); Va. Code Ann. § 6.1-377 (1983); Wis. Stat. Ann. § 103.13(2) (West 1986).
10. *Privacy Times*, Mar. 2, 1983.
11. David Linowes, *Privacy in America* (Univ. of Illinois Press, 1989).
12. *Privacy Times*, Mar. 2, 1983.
13. *Privacy Times*, Jan. 19, 1982.

14. *Privacy Times*, Nov. 17, 1982.
15. Access Reports/Privacy, February 26, 1980.
16. W. Prosser, "Privacy," 48 Calif. L. Rev. 383, 389 (1960). *See also* Restatement (Second) of Torts 652C.
17. *Levias v. United Airlines*, 27 Ohio App. 3d 222, 5000 N.E.2d 370 (1985).
18. *Bratt v. IBM* 785F.2d 352, 359 (1st Cir. 1986).
19. *Eddy v. Brown*: 715 P.2d 74 (Oklahoma 1986).
20. *Employers Face Upsurge in Suits over Defamation*, 9(34) *Nat. Law. J.*, 1 (May 4, 1987).
21. *Wanda L. Robinson v. The Chesapeake and Potomac Telephone Co.*, No. 81-1227, Slip. op., (July 27, 1984), U.S. District Court, District of Columbia.
22. *Detroit Edison v. NLRB*, 440 U.S. 301 (1979).
23. *Westinghouse Electric Corp. v. NIOSH*, 638 F.2d 570 (3d Cir. 1980).
24. BNA Study, 87.
25. N.J. Bell Tel. Co. & Comm. Workers of Amer., Local 1023: 265 NLRB No. 180 (Dec. 16, 1982).
26. *Salt River Valley Water Users' Ass'n. & International Brotherhood of Elec. Workers, et al*: 272 NLRB No. 52 (Sept. 28, 1984).
27. Privacy Protection Study Commission, *Personal Privacy in an Information Society* (1977).
28. Office of Technology Assessment, *The Electronic Supervisor: New Technology, New Tensions* (Government Printing Office, 1987).
29. *Id.*
30. *Id.*
31. *Id.*
32. *Privacy Times*, Nov. 21, 1984.
33. *Computer Monitoring and Other Dirty Tricks*, 9 to 5, National Association of Working Women, SEIU (1986).
34. *Id.*
35. *Watkins v. L. M. Berry*, 704 F.2d 579 (11th. Cir. 1983).
36. *Briggs v. American Filter Co.*, 704 F.2d 577 (11th. Cir. 1983).
37. *Privacy Times*, July 20, 1987.
38. 162 Cal. App. 3d 241, 208 Cal. Rptr. 524 (1984).
39. *Privacy Times*, Nov. 12, 1987.
40. *Privacy Times*, June 10, 1988.
41. *Simmer, Secretary of Transportation et al. v. Railway Labor Executives Ass'n. et al.* No. 87-1555 slip op. (U.S. Mar. 21, 1988).

42. *National Treasury Employees Union et al. v. Von Raab* (Commissioner, U.S. Customs Service), No. 86-1879 slip op. (U.S. Mar. 21, 1989).
43. Interview with staff member of Senate Committee on Labor & Human Resources, Aug. 1988.

X

Credit Records and Consumer Reports

What is a "credit record"?
The term "credit record," in its narrow sense, refers to information describing a person's previous financial transactions which bear on his present creditworthiness. But in its broader and more commonly used sense, the term refers to any information describing a person's financial and employment history, state of health, character, reputation, and style of living that may be used in deciding whether to give that person a loan, credit, an insurance policy, a job, a professional or business license, or some other commercial benefit.

The Privacy Commission described six types of information generally found in credit reports.

1. *Identifying information:* name and spouse's name, Social Security number, address and telephone number;
2. *Financial status:* amount of income (present and past), employer (present and past), occupation, sources of income;
3. *Credit history:* previous types, extent, and sources of credit granted;
4. *Existing lines of credit:* payment habits, outstanding obligations and debts, extent of current lines of credit;
5. *Public Record Information:* lawsuits, judgments, tax liens, bankruptcies, arrests, convictions (TRW has a policy of not including pending lawsuit or criminal history items);
6. *Prior requesters:* names of subscribers who requested information on the individual in the past.

While individually many of these items are not particularly sensitive, together they reveal a lot about a person's lifestyle and habits. Credit bureaus can track individuals as they move from neighborhoods, jobs, lifestyles, and income levels.

Credit reports are compiled primarily by credit bureaus, investigative-reporting agencies, and private-detective agencies, which sell their services to "subscribers"—creditors, employers, and insurers who need to make background checks on prospective borrowers, employees, and policyholders. Merchants' protective associations, cooperative loan exchanges, and other nonprofit groups may also perform credit-reporting services without charge or at a nominal fee for their members. All these agencies and organizations maintain permanent, often computerized records on the subjects of their investigations, and many are affiliated in local, regional, or national associations that exchange credit records among their members.

A leading reporting agency is Equifax, Inc., also known as CBI, Inc., with headquarters in Atlanta, Georgia. At any one time, Equifax has files on millions of individuals nationwide.[1] Of two thousand credit bureaus, the five largest maintain a total of 250 million credit records.[2] TRW, Inc., another giant credit bureau based in California, keeps computerized data on 140 million individuals. The industry as a whole is estimated to gross over $1 billion a year in revenues and to keep files on over 200 million people. Anyone who has ever applied for a job, an insurance policy, or a loan or credit is likely to be the subject of one of those files.

The investigation conducted by a reporting agency may be limited to the formal records of a person's financial resources and history: sources of income, payment of bills, bad debts, bankruptcies, suits, garnishments, tax liens, etc. A simple credit report of this kind is most often required for a loan or a credit card. But the inquiry may go beyond this, to include interviews with neighbors, employers, landlords, family, and friends for information about the person's lifestyle, character, and general reputation within the community, as well as contacts with the police, doctors, hospitals, insurance companies, and schools. These more wide-ranging searches are called investigative reports and are frequently conducted for prospective employers and insurers.

Both simple credit reports and the broader investigative reports — together known under the general term "consumer reports" — are regulated by a federal statute called the Fair Credit Reporting Act of 1970 (FCRA).[3] In addition nineteen states have credit-reporting statutes similar to the federal law. A few states have enacted laws that place more stringent restrictions on the operations of consumer-reporting agencies.[4]

Which records are regulated by the Fair Credit Reporting Act?

The FCRA applies only to records containing information about an individual (not a business) and intended for use in decisions concerning the granting of:

1. personal credit;
2. personal, family, or household insurance;
3. employment;
4. a license or other government benefit for which consideration of a person's financial responsibility or status is required by law;
5. any other "legitimate business need" involving a business transaction with the individual — for example, the renting of an apartment to a tenant.

The act applies only to information collected and transmitted by a third party.[5] Thus, a reference given directly by a former employer to a prospective employer, describing his own personal experience with an individual, is not a consumer report within the meaning of the statute. Nor is a direct communication from department store A to department store B, describing how prompt or delinquent a particular customer has been in paying bills at department store A. But if an outside agency transmits that information from a former to a prospective employer, or from store A to store B, it becomes a consumer report under the FCRA.

Both the courts and the Federal Trade Commission (FTC), which has responsibility for the administrative enforcement of the statute, have attempted to clarify specific kinds of reports to which the FCRA applies, often with confusing or contradictory results. For example, under a formal interpretation issued by the FTC, the US Office of Personnel Management, although it collects and disseminates information on current and prospective employees of the federal government in much the same way that a credit-reporting agency might handle such information, does not fall within the scope of FCRA. While a US district court in California ruled the FCRA applicable to a report compiled in connection with the payment of an insurance claim,[6] the FTC interpreted the act as inapplicable to such reports, except when they are later used in a decision to cancel, refuse to renew, or increase the premiums for an insurance policy.[7] The act has been held by a state court in Washington to cover a report originally compiled for a personal health-insurance policy when it was later used again for a business insurance policy.[8] In a much-disputed interpretation by a US district court in Georgia, it was held not to cover the report of a polygraph test transmitted by a polygraph examiner to a prospective employer.[9]

Because these and other cases involving the FCRA's coverage are unclear and because the legislative history suggests that Congress intended a broad rather than a restrictive interpretation, for practical purposes it is best to assume that if a report was compiled or used for any of the five general purposes enumerated above, it falls within the scope of the act.

Is there any restriction on the kinds of information that may be contained in a credit report?

The federal statute forbids only certain "obsolete information." It is the absence of any effective restriction on the contents of credit records that accounts for the most serious abuses of privacy in consumer reporting. The FCRA requires in general that agencies implement "reasonable procedures" (undefined) to assure the accuracy of information[10] but has nothing to say about the propriety or relevance of information. Many reports contain items about people's sex lives, drinking habits, housekeeping standards, politics, social relationships, and marital problems. Even if such items are no more than unsubstantiated tidbits of malicious neighborhood gossip, the FCRA does not prevent their dissemination to would-be employers or creditors. In fact, inclusion of information about the most private areas of a person's life is routine in most investigative reports. (Simple credit reports tend to concentrate on the objective records of one's financial dealings although there are exceptions.)

The FCRA does place time limits on the reporting of certain kinds of "adverse information."[11] Adverse information obtained from field investigations and interviews is not supposed to be included in a report if it has not been received or verified within the last three months. Bankruptcies more than fourteen years old may not be reported. Suits, tax liens, and accounts placed for collection may not be reported after seven years. Arrests, indictments, and convictions may not be reported more than seven years after disposition, release, or parole. Seven years is also the limit on all "other adverse information." But even these restrictions do not apply if a report is to be used in connection with credit or insurance of $50,000 or more or employment at a salary of $20,000 or more.

Under some state fair-credit-reporting acts, notably those in New York and Maine,[12] time limits are placed on other items, and certain kinds of information are barred altogether. New York, for example, does not permit a consumer-reporting agency to report an arrest or criminal charge not followed by a conviction, unless charges are still pending. Nor may it handle information relating to a person's race, religion, color, ancestry, or ethnic origin, or any information "which it has reason to know is inaccurate." For most purposes, information relating to drug or alcohol addiction or confinement in a mental institution may not be reported after seven years. In addition to these restrictions, Maine requires that all information be "reasonably relevant to the purpose for which it is sought" and bans reports dealing with a person's political affiliation or characterizing his personal lifestyle. A few other states forbid the reporting of arrests and indictments not followed by conviction.[13]

It is important to understand that these restrictions apply only to reports made by consumer-reporting agencies. Except where other laws or regulations forbid it, an insurer, creditor, employer, or licensing body might be able to obtain such information from another source.

Can a consumer-reporting agency get information from records that are legally confidential?

Yes. Applicants for employment, insurance, credit, licenses, and other benefits are frequently asked to sign a waiver of confidentiality or authorization of access that is so broadly worded that it applies to virtually all personal records. Armed with such a waiver, the reporting agency may be able to obtain access to all kinds of confidential records, including hospital, police, and school records. Most people do not realize the significance of what they are signing, and those who do may be afraid to refuse for fear of losing the job or benefits they are trying to obtain. Although some custodians of these confidential records may refuse to honor a general waiver and insist upon a specific authorization for the release of designated records, few can be counted upon to do so. It is difficult to resist a demand that one sign a general waiver of confidentiality. In some circumstances it may be possible to ask for an enumeration of the specific records that will be sought and to reword the authorization accordingly. It may also be feasible to place a termination date upon the authorization—say 30 or 60 days hence—so that it cannot be filed away and reused.

Another method by which consumer-reporting agencies get legally confidential information is by obtaining it from a source other than a confidential record. The most common example of this practice is the arrest record. In many jurisdictions, law enforcement agencies are prohibited by law or regulation from giving out information on a particular person's past arrests. But the police blotter—the day-to-day compilation of arrests maintained at the precinct house or police headquarters—is a public record, and in many communities it is published in its entirety in the daily paper. Local consumer-reporting agencies often clip these listings and index them for use in future reports. When local agencies are linked into regional or national associations, such records can be disseminated far beyond the community where the arrest took place. Of course, the blotter does not contain information on the disposition of the arrest, such as later dismissal of charges or acquittal, and so neither does the report that goes to the employer or insurer.

Finally, there have been a few instances in which consumer-reporting agencies obtained confidential records by deception or fraud. For example, the investigator may represent himself as a doctor in a telephone call to the medical-records department of a hospital or even show up dressed in a white coat. Occasionally, an investigator may have a friend in the police department or hospital-records room who simply hands over any information he asks for. Many of these practices are legally prohibited;[14] others have not yet been addressed by legislation.

How does a person know if he is the subject of a consumer report or if a report will be compiled?

The only sure way to find out if such a report exists would be to write to every investigative-reporting agency, credit bureau, loan exchange, merchants' association, and private detective agency—obviously an impossibility. Because the FCRA does not require a consumer-reporting agency to notify every individual on whom it opens a file, most people remain unaware of the existence of such reports until after they have been turned down for a loan, job, or insurance policy and have been told that it was because of "adverse information" in a consumer report.

The FCRA does not require a report user (that is, the employer, creditor, or insurer who will use the information to make a decision about an individual) to tell an applicant that a simple credit report has been or will be compiled. Only when the user wants a full investigative report—one involving interviews with third parties to determine reputation, living style, and so forth—must he provide prior written notification to the subject. (An exception to the notification requirement is for an investigative report to be used for employment in a position for which the person has not specifically applied. Thus, a person's life can be subjected to covert scrutiny merely because an employer may have an interest in him, even though he has expressed no interest in the employer. This is the "headhunter" exception, created for executive-search agencies.) The required notification is usually placed somewhere on the insurance, credit, or employment application and is often couched in very general language. The applicant has the right to request and receive a more "complete and accurate" written description of the "nature and scope" of the investigation but still won't know which reporting agency will be making the report.[15] (The applicant may attempt, at this point, to obtain an enumeration of specific records that will be sought and persons who will be contacted as a part of the investigation, as was discussed above in connection with general waivers of confidentiality. The statute does not say exactly what constitutes a "complete and accurate" description.)

If the employment, insurance, credit, or other benefit is refused, or if the credit or insurance is offered at an increased charge, and if this decision is based partly or wholly upon information in a consumer report, the report user must reveal to the subject the name and address of the reporting agency.[16]

As a practical matter, then, a person will ordinarily learn about his credit record only after the information in it has been used to make an adverse decision about him.

What if an adverse decision is based on information not obtained from a consumer-reporting agency?

If credit for personal, family, or household purposes is denied or the charges for such credit increased, and if that action is based wholly or in part on information obtained from a source other than a consumer-reporting agency, the FCRA requires that the creditor disclose the reasons for the decision if the credit applicant submits a written request within sixty days after learning of the decision. The creditor must inform the applicant of his right to submit such a request when the adverse decision is made known to him.[17] This provision for notification does not apply, however, to adverse decisions involving employment or insurance.

Do credit bureaus receive data from the federal government?

Yes, since 1983. Prior to then, credit bureaus were reluctant to accept data on debtors from federal agencies because the Justice Department said that such sharing would make the credit bureau "federal contractors," thus requiring them to comply with the additional data collection, management, and disclosure rules of the Privacy Act. Credit bureaus did not want to shoulder the extra burden. But Congress, intent on improving the government's debt collection abilities, concluded it was important that those who did not repay government loans be reported to private credit bureaus so their credit ratings would suffer. In 1982, it enacted the Debt Collection Practices Act, amending the Privacy Act to clarify that credit bureaus would not be deemed "federal contractors" for accepting debtor data from federal agencies. Two years later, the Office of Management and Budget created a computer link between federal debtor files and credit bureaus to facilitate a more efficient exchange of data.

The amendment also changed the confidentiality rules of the US Tax Code to permit the Internal Revenue Service to provide lending agencies with data on outstanding tax liabilities, penalties, interest, and fines on loan applicants.

Moreover, it permitted the IRS to divulge taxpayer mailing addresses to locate federal debtors.

In 1989 a controversy surfaced regarding a proposal by TRW, Inc. to pay the Social Security Administration $1 million to verify its computerized list of 140 million Social Security numbers. In previous years, the SSA had run a "test run" of a tape containing 130,000 Social Security numbers. But the SSA decided against the TRW proposal after it was criticized by lawmakers and privacy advocates (see chapter 6 on Social Security numbers).

Does the government have access to consumer reports?

Yes. A government agency may obtain a consumer report like any other employer, insurer, or creditor. It may also obtain a report if it is required by law to consider a person's financial responsibility or status before granting a license or other benefit. When a government agency obtains a report for these purposes, it is bound by the rules and restrictions the FCRA places upon all users of consumer reports.

But the FCRA also permits consumer-reporting agencies to give some information to a government agency for other purposes. Upon the government's request, it may reveal the following: a person's name, address, former address, and present and former places of employment.[18] Thus, if a government agency is looking for a fugitive from justice, it can obtain this "identifying information" from a consumer-reporting agency's files.

The statute leaves to the consumer-reporting agency the responsibility for determining whether a government agency's request is for a "permissible purpose" (thus qualifying for a full consumer report) or for some other purpose (thus limited to identifying information). That determination will rest heavily upon what the government chooses to tell the reporting agency. In practice, it is unlikely that a consumer-reporting agency will very strongly resist a government demand for more than mere identifying information. It must also be remembered that even if a government agency is stymied in its attempt to get certain information from a consumer-reporting agency, it may be successful in obtaining the same information directly from an employer, credit-card company, bank, insurance company, hospital, or other such record custodian.

Aside from the special provisions applying to government agencies, can anyone at all obtain information from a consumer-reporting agency?

Not legally. Despite these provisions, credit bureaus are not considered very secure. In 1984, for instance, TRW learned belatedly that computer hackers from around the country had been penetrating its mammoth databank on ninety million consumers. Apparently an access code was leaked or stolen from a Sears store in Sacramento, California, and posted on an electronic bulletin board. TRW had no idea how many confidential records were read by hackers or to what extent they committed credit fraud.[19] Months later, Burt Mazelow, a California resident claiming that he suffered "shock, grievous pain and suffering" because unauthorized outsiders had seen his credit records, sued TRW for being negligent about safeguarding confidential data. The suit was dismissed.[20]

In 1988 the House Armed Services Subcommittee on Investigations reported that "hostile intelligence agencies" were finding private credit bureaus to be a rich source for leads on individuals with access to US government secrets who might be experiencing financial problems. "DOD [Department of Defense] officials advised that one way in which hostile intelligence agents select potential targets (for espionage) is by obtaining personal information through nationwide credit data systems. There are at least five major companies who maintain voluminous amounts of personal information on a large segment of society," the report said, referring to Credit Bureau, Inc., TRW, Inc., Chilton Corp., Trans Union Credit Information Co., and Associated Credit Bureaus. The report suggested that national security was jeopardized by the credit bureaus' practice of collecting more kinds of data and by the ineffectiveness of credit privacy safeguards.[21]

Agencies are permitted to prepare and disseminate reports only for the "permissible purposes" enumerated in the FCRA: for use in decisions concerning the granting of credit, insurance, employment, license or other government benefit, or for other "legitimate business need" in connection with a business transaction involving the subject of the report. The agency must take reasonable measures to verify the identity of report users and to assure that a report will be used only for a permissible purpose.[22] The FCRA provides for criminal penalties—up to $5000 or a year in prison or both—for anyone who obtains information from a consumer-reporting agency "under false pretenses"[23] (for example, someone who poses as a prospective employer) or for an employee of a consumer-reporting agency who "knowingly and willfully" provides information to an unauthorized recipient.[24]

May people learn the contents of their own credit records?

Yes, up to a point. The FCRA says that a person, upon request to the consumer-reporting agency, must be told "the nature and substance" of the information in his record.[25] This means the person need not be allowed to read the record for himself, have it read to him word for word, or obtain a copy of it. Under some state statutes, however, a person may either read or obtain a copy of his records or both.[26]

Two kinds of information in a credit record need not be revealed to the subject under the FCRA. One is medical information obtained from physicians, hospitals, and other medical personnel and facilities.[27] The other is the identity of the sources of information collected solely for use in an investigative report.[28] (Sources of information used in a simple credit report are subject to disclosure.) For example, if in an interview for an investigative report a neighbor said that the subject is a drug user or has a reputation for cheating on his wife, the neighbor's identity as the source of that information would not be revealed except by court order.

The agency must reveal to the subject the names of any recipient of a report on him within the last two years for employment purposes or within the last six months for any other purpose.[29]

How can people examine their credit records?

A consumer-reporting agency must respond to a person's request for access to his own records during normal business hours and upon "reasonable notice." The individual may appear in person or may request disclosure by telephone. He must furnish personal identification and may be accompanied by one other person of his own choosing. Telephone and travel costs are borne by the individual.[30]

The agency is obliged, under the FCRA, to provide trained personnel to explain the contents of the record.[31] However, many people report that they have encountered agency employees who are poorly prepared, even openly hostile and obstructive, and in the absence of a statutory right of physical access to one's own record or to a copy of its contents (available only in a few states), there is no sure way of judging whether the agency's oral summary is either accurate or complete.

The agency may charge a "reasonable fee" for disclosing the contents of a record to the subject. The fee must be specified before the interview. An exception is made for people who request access to their records within thirty days of an adverse decision (such as denial of employment or an increase in insurance rates) resulting from information in a consumer report. In such cases, no charge may be levied.[32]

In spite of the difficulties, frustrations, and expenses, it is important to examine the contents of one's credit records. Consumer reports are known to have a high incidence of inaccurate, incomplete, and misleading information. It has been charged that certain consumer-reporting agencies set quotas of "adverse" reports for their agents—that is, the agent must come up with derogatory information in a certain percentage of his investigations. It has also been charged that some agencies conduct haphazard investigations and fill their reports with a lot of unverified, even invented, data, a result of the enormous daily and weekly quotas that each agency investigator is expected to complete.[33] The trouble and expense of obtaining access to one's credit records are well worthwhile if measured against the risk of needlessly losing a job, loan, or insurance policy.

Can anything be done if the information in a credit record is inaccurate?

Yes. Under the FCRA, if an item appears to be inaccurate or incomplete, the subject may so inform the agency, and the agency must reinvestigate the item within a "reasonable period of time." However, the agency may refuse to reinvestigate if it believes the dispute to be "frivolous" or "irrelevant."[34] The act does not specify just what such reinvestigation entails: in practice, it may turn out to be no more than a renewed query to the original source of the information.

(Under Maine's more stringent provisions for reinvestigations, the agency must note in the record what steps it took to reinvestigate a disputed item.)[35] Nor does the FCRA define how an agency may decide to dismiss a request as "frivolous," except to say that the mere presence of contradictory information in the record "does not in and of itself constitute reasonable grounds" for such a judgment.[36] Obviously, a great deal of scope is left to the agency's discretion.

If the agency cannot verify the disputed information, it is supposed to delete it from the records. If no such correction is made, the subject may enter into the records a brief statement of his own version of the story, and in subsequent disseminations of the information, the fact that the item is in dispute must be clearly noted, and the subject's statement or a summary of it must be included. But again, if the agency considers the dispute "frivolous," it may refuse to accept the statement into the record. The agency may limit the statement to one hundred words if it helps the person write a clear summary of the dispute.[37]

The subject also has the right to demand that previous recipients of the disputed information be informed of the correction or be given the explanatory statement. The agency must, at minimum, inform any person who received the disputed information for employment purposes within the last two years or for any other purpose within the last six months.[38] The agency may not charge a fee for notifying previous recipients of an item that was found to be inaccurate or could not be verified nor for transmitting to such recipients the subject's explanatory statement if he has suffered an "adverse action" based on a consumer report within the last thirty days. In other circumstances, a fee may be charged, so long as the subject is told ahead of time what the fee will be.[39]

Can a consumer-reporting agency be sued for invading a person's privacy, for disseminating false or damaging information, or for violating a person's rights under a fair-credit-reporting statute?

Yes, but with difficulty. Under the federal statute, a consumer-reporting agency, the user of a report, or a person furnishing information for a report may be sued for defamation, invasion of privacy, or negligence only with respect to "false information furnished with malice or willful intent to injure."[40] Because it is very difficult to prove actual malice and willful intent, such suits are extremely hard to win. The only state statutes that do not effectively immunize agencies, users, and sources from defamation and invasion of privacy suits are those in Montana, Maine, and New York.[41]

The FCRA permits suits against a consumer-reporting agency or report user for willful noncompliance or negligent noncompliance with any requirement of the act. In the case of willful noncompliance, the injured person may be awarded actual damages, punitive damages, and costs and attorneys' fees.[42] For negligent noncompliance, the court may award actual damages and costs and attorneys' fees.[43] The obstacle here is that reporting agencies and users can defend against negligence suits by demonstrating that they took "reasonable procedures" to comply with the statute. Because the act does not define or specify any "reasonable procedures," the showing of a "good faith effort" on the part of the agency may be enough for a successful defense.

Civil suits under the FCRA may be brought in a US district court or other court of competent jurisdiction. There is a two-year statute of limitations. However, when a defendant reporting agency or report user has willfully misrepresented information and when that information is material to the case against the agency or user, the two-year period does not begin until the discovery of the misrepresentation.[44]

How have the courts interpreted the FCRA?

First, there has not been a great deal of litigation since most people are not willing to make the necessary investment to sue a credit bureau over a problem with records. Second, as noted earlier, there has been inconsistency among the courts in deciding what kinds of files are "consumer reports." For instance, while a federal court in California ruled that a report prepared in connection with an insurance claim was covered by the act, a judge in Georgia said that it was not. Files prepared for state physician licensing boards and motor vehicle records used for insurance purposes have been deemed to fall within the act's jurisdiction, while employment-related polygraph exams, background investigations for lobbyists, and reports prepared for child support actions have been ruled outside of the FCRA's scope.[45] None of these basic inconsistencies have risen to the level of Supreme Court review. Moreover, as of August 1989, Congress has never held an oversight hearing, and the FTC has done a weak job of overseeing and enforcing the law.

Nonetheless, some important trends have emerged from the case law. They fall into the following categories:

Reasonable procedures.   The FCRA requires credit bureaus to use "reasonable procedures" to insure the "maximum possible accuracy." The courts have failed to define "reasonableness" concretely for collecting data from merchants or through neighborhood interviews.

In one case, a consumer sued Equifax for inaccurately describing his job to an insurance company, causing the denial of disability benefits. The Equifax investigator had spoken to "reliable sources" and arrived at a mistaken conclusion about the man's job description. A federal appeals court, while acknowledging the crucial inaccuracy, said Equifax's policy of conducting interviews was not "negligent" and dismissed the suit without indicating what would constitute unreasonable interviewing or investigating techniques.[46]

In another case, the same appeals court ruled that another consumer agency failed to use reasonable procedures when its report labeled St. Louis news reporter James Millstone "a hippie" and "suspected drug user" and caused an initial denial of his auto insurance policy. Millstone's lawsuit revealed that the judgment was based on a thirty-minute interview with a former—soon afterwards deceased—neighbor. The reporting agency made no attempts to verify the data and repeatedly denied Millstone's access to his records. The court called the agency's methods "slipshod and slovenly" and awarded Millstone $25,000 in punitive damages, $2,500 in actual damages and $12,500 for costs and attorneys' fees.[47]

In yet another instance, a consumer complained to a credit bureau that it had received inaccurate information from a merchant and reported it. But the credit bureau merely rechecked the data with the merchant. A court ruled that a more thorough reinvestigation was required.[48] Similarly courts have ruled that credit bureaus that permit merchants direct access and entry capabilities fail to maximize accuracy when they do not include procedures to verify the data.[49]

Accuracy of data.   Courts have held that certain numerical ratings used by credit bureaus, although "technically accurate," do not meet the accuracy standards of the FCRA. A Virginia man once learned that he was denied a credit card because the bureau rated him a "19"—meaning the bank either wrote off a loan as a bad debt or the man skipped town—and a "0"—meaning the balance was zero. In fact, the credit report failed to show that the man had paid off the loan after it was written off as a bad debt. A federal appeals panel said the bits of data, while accurate, actually gave a misleading picture.[50]

On the other hand, a Georgia court ruled that recovery under the FCRA requires a clear misstatement or inaccuracy in the credit agency's report. In this case, a man was denied a loan because his credit report showed he was involved in litigation. What it failed to explain was that the man was in court in his official capacity as a county deputy marshall. His complaint against the credit bureau was dismissed.[51]

Collecting data under false pretense.   The FCRA provides a civil right of action against a user of credit information for obtaining such information under false pretenses, the US Court of Appeals for the Sixth Circuit ruled in 1984.[52]

Damages.   When consumers are able to show clear violations of the law that damage them, courts have upheld damages awards against credit bureaus. When a bureau failed to respond to a consumer's complaint that his report incorrectly showed he was the defendant (instead of the plaintiff) in a civil action, the court approved a jury award of $200,000 in punitive and actual damages.[53] Even when there are no out-of-pocket losses, a consumer can still get damages for mental distress and for injury to reputation, family, sense of well-being, and creditworthiness.[54]

Considering these pro-consumer court rulings, has the FCRA achieved its goal of giving consumers adequate controls over their credit data?

No. There are a number of reasons:

1. The consumer is burdened with taking the time and traveling the distance to the credit bureau, particularly a problem if it is not a local bureau. Telephone contact may be made, but bureaus have been crit-

icized for having too few operators and operators who inform the consumers of their rights inadequately.

2. Consumers do not have the right to see their credit files, but only the right to know their nature and substance. In practice, many credit bureaus do provide a copy of the credit report, but this is of no help if the problem was an inaccurate match so that the requester received an entirely different report or the report has since been updated and the offending information changed.

3. The FCRA vests a lot of initial discretion in the credit bureaus to dismiss consumer complaints as frivolous.

4. The FCRA defines no standards for an adequate reinvestigation.

5. If the information remains disputed, credit bureaus do not have to include the consumer's statement. Many credit bureaus just note that the item is disputed.

6. Even if the information is correct in the initial credit bureau's report, it remains uncorrected in all the places it has been sent, including other credit bureaus. The FCRA only requires that credit bureaus honor requests for dissemination of the corrected report to persons who received a report within the past six months.

7. The FTC has not enforced the law aggressively.

What other laws regulate credit reports?

The Equal Credit Opportunity Act[55] prohibits credit grantors from using a person's race, sex, marital status, and certain other potentially discriminatory standards in making decisions on the extension of loans or credit. This does not necessarily mean that such items won't continue to be noted in a person's credit records, however, since the law forbids only their use by the creditor, not their collection by a consumer-reporting agency.

The Fair Credit Billing Act[56] forbids the reporting of a disputed bill as a "delinquent account" for the ninety days during which a person may withhold a disputed payment. This does have a direct effect on credit records because the notation of a delinquency in a consumer report usually results in the refusal of further credit. The statute requires that such accounts be reported as disputed or, after ninety days, as both disputed and delinquent; within the ninety-day period, no creditor may use a disputed account as grounds for refusing credit or a loan.

Both the Equal Credit Opportunity Act and the Fair Credit Billing Act apply only to the uses of information by creditors. Neither places restrictions on employers, insurers, or other consumer-report users.

NOTES

1. Privacy Protection Study Commission, *Personal Privacy in an Information Society*, 325–26 (U.S. Government Printing Office, July 1977).
2. *Id.* 55–56.
3. 15 U.S.C. § 1681 *et seq.*
4. 15 U.S.C. § 1681a.
5. 16 C.F.R. § 600.6.
6. *Beresh v. Retail Credit Co.*, 358 F. Supp. 260 (C.D. Cal., 1973).
7. Bureau of Consumer Protection, Division of Consumer Credit, Federal Trade Commission, *Compliance with the Fair Credit Reporting Act*, 46–47 (2d ed., rev., January 1977).
8. *Rasor v. Retail Credit Co.*, 554 P.2d 1041 (Wash., 1976).
9. *Peller v. Retail Credit Co.*, 359 F. Supp. 1235 (N.D. Ga., 1973); aff'd 505 F.2d 733 (5th Cir., 1974).
10. 15 U.S.C. 1681e(b). The best-known case addressing the definition of "reasonable procedures" is *Miller v. Credit Bureau*, No. SC-29451-71, CCH Consumer Credit Guide, Para. 99, 173 (D.C. Super. Ct., 1972).
11. 15 U.S.C. § 1681c.
12. N.Y. Gen. Bus. Law § 380; Me. Rev. Stat. Ann. tit. 10, § 1312.
13. *See* Cal. Civ. Code § 1785–1786; N.M. Stat. Ann. § 50-8-1 *et seq.*; Ky. Rev. Stat. § 331.350.
14. *E.g.*, there are numerous statutes and regulations restricting persons to whom arrest and conviction records, medical records, school records, etc., may be released. However, pretext interviews — in which the interviewer misrepresents his identity or the purpose of the interview — are not now illegal.
15. 15 U.S.C. § 1681d.
16. 15 U.S.C. § 1681m(a).

17. 15 U.S.C. § 1681m(b).
18. 15 U.S.C. § 1681f.
19. *Privacy Times*, July 6, 1984.
20. *Privacy Times*, Nov. 7, 1988.
21. *Privacy Times*, Jan. 20, 1988.
22. 15 U.S.C. § 1681e(a).
23. 15 U.S.C. § 1681q.
24. 15 U.S.C. § 1681r.
25. 15 U.S.C. § 1681g.
26. *See, e.g.*, Okla. Stat. Ann. tit. 24, §§ 81–85; Md. Com. Law 14-1201 *et seq.*; Ariz. Rev. Stat. Ann. § 44-1691 *et seq.*; N.Y. Gen. Bus. Law, *supra* note 12; Me. Rev. Stat. Ann. *supra* note 12; Cal. Civ. Code, *supra* note 13.
27. 15 U.S.C. § 1681g(a)(1).
28. 15 U.S.C. § g(a)(2).
29. 15 U.S.C. § 1681g(a)(3).
30. 15 U.S.C. § 1681h(a) and (b).
31. 15 U.S.C. § 1681h(c).
32. 15 U.S.C. § 1681j.
33. Privacy Protection Study Commission, *supra* note 1, ch. 8.
34. 15 U.S.C. § 1681i(a).
35. Me. Rev. Stat. Ann., *supra* note 12.
36. 15 U.S.C. § 1681i(a).
37. 15 U.S.C. § 1681i(a), (b), and (c).
38. 15 U.S.C. § 1681i(d).
39. 15 U.S.C. § 1681j.
40. 15 U.S.C. § 1681h(e).
41. Mont. Codes Ann. 18-501 *et seq.*; Me Rev. Stat. Ann., *supra* note 12; N.Y. Gen. Bus. Law, *supra* note 12.
42. 15 U.S.C. § 1681n.
43. 15 U.S.C. § 1688o.
44. 15 U.S.C. § 1681p.
45. *Privacy Times*, July 7, 1981.
46. *Hauser v. Equifax, Inc.*, 608 F2d 811 (8th Cir. 1979).
47. *Millstone v. O'Hanlon*, 528 F.2d 829 (8th Cir. 1976).
48. *Bryant v. TRW*, 6890 F.2d 72 (6th Cir. 1982).
49. *Lowry v. Credit Bureau of Georgia*, 444 F. Supp. 541 (N.D. Ga. 1978) and *Thompson v. San Antonio Retail Merchants' Ass'n.*, 682 F.2d 509 (5th Cir. 1982).
50. *Koropoulos et al. v. The Credit Bureau Inc.* 734 F.2d 37 D.C. Cir. 1984.
51. *Austin v. Bankamerica Service Corp.* 419 F. Supp. 730 N.D. Ga. 1974.

52. *Jean and Sailor Kennedy v. Border City Savings & Loan Ass'n.*, No. 83-3380, slip op. at Ca-6 (Nov. 1, 1984).
53. *Pinner v. Schmidt*, 617 F. Supp. 342 (D.C. La. 1985).
54. *Fischl v. General Motors Acceptance Corp.*: 708 F.2d 143 (C.A. La. 1983) and *Morris v. Credit Bureau of Cincinnati Inc.* 563 F. Supp. 962 (D.C. Ohio 1983).
55. 15 U.S.C. § 1691.
56. 15 U.S.C. § 1666–1666j.

XI

Financial and Tax Records

The area of personal financial information illustrates the classic tension between the individual's right to privacy and law enforcement's need for access to potentially vital evidence. On one hand, the individual's privacy interest in bank records is strong, given that a record of check and credit card transactions provides the best description of movements, purchases, consumption habits, reading and other leisure preferences, and associations. It is not surprising that personal financial information usually is the lifeblood of successful law enforcement investigations. The law enforcement interest in financial data has increased due to the boom in the illegal drug industry and the ability of drug barons to "launder" large sums of cash through banks, real estate, and other transactions. While the right to privacy has received important judicial and legislative concessions, the clear trend has been to favor law enforcers' authority to see personal financial data.

Should people assume that their bank records are confidential?

No. Despite a common presumption to the contrary, the records maintained by banks describing the financial affairs of a customer—deposits, withdrawals, checks, interest payments, loans, overdrafts, and so on—do not "belong" to the customer. In 1976, the US Supreme Court ruled these records are merely the records of commercial transactions, not confidential communications; and they are the bank's, not the customer's. For these reasons, a bank customer has no constitutionally "legitimate expectation of privacy" in his or her bank records and no legal "standing" to prevent the bank from revealing the records to others.[1] Bank records are confidential only to the extent that federal and state statutes forbid certain government officials or private parties from obtaining access to them without a customer's consent.

The most central of these statutes is the Right to Financial Privacy Act of 1978 (RFPA), a direct response to the Supreme

Court's *Miller* decision, which set procedures for federal agents' access to personal financial files. The RFPA and similar state statutes are limited in their scope, and where they do not reach the confidentiality of a person's bank records is at the mercy of the bank's discretion. Fortunately, many major banks have established strong confidentiality policies for customer records. However, a bank's discretion is shaped by legal record-keeping and -reporting requirements, notably under the Bank Secrecy Act, that require storage of personal financial data.

Why do government agencies seek access to bank records?

Bank records are often used by the police, prosecutors, and other law-enforcement officials in criminal investigations. Until the enactment of the federal Right to Financial Privacy Act in 1978, FBI agents usually were able to obtain a customer's bank records merely by presenting themselves to a bank's security chief and announcing that an investigation in progress required the records of a certain customer or even a search through the records of many customers. Such informal examination of bank records was a common occurrence in official surveillance of antiwar and civil-rights organizations and "radical" political parties of both right and left in the 1950s and 1960s, and early 1970s. Except in a few states that have enacted their own bank privacy laws, local and state law-enforcement officials are still free to rummage through a bank customer's records in this manner. Local, state, and federal tax authorities and other agencies charged with the enforcement of tax, securities, and financial laws naturally find personal bank records useful, either in their routine administrative procedures or in criminal investigations. And Bank Secrecy Act record-keeping requirements are intended to increase the amount of personal bank information available to these agencies because such records "have a high degree of usefulness in criminal, tax, and regulatory investigations and proceedings."[2]

Determination of an individual's eligibility for a government benefit or participation in a government program often involves an examination of bank records. This is usually done with the individual's written consent, although one really has little choice in the matter and often is obliged to authorize access to all personal bank records rather than to specific information.

How does the federal Right to Financial Privacy Act protect bank customers against government access to their records?

The Right to Financial Privacy Act forbids an official or employee of a federal agency to obtain or examine the bank records of any person without that person's consent, except pursuant to formal legal processes—an administrative subpoena or summons, a search warrant, a judicial subpoena (court order), or a formal written request.[3] (The provision for a "formal written request" is limited to agencies that do not have the authority to issue administrative subpoenas or summonses.) It is important to bear in mind that the act applies only to federal, not state or local, officials. Therefore, its strictures apply to agents of the FBI, investigators of the Justice and Treasury Departments, and employees of the Social Security Administration, for example, but not to local or state tax-agency investigators, welfare administrators, or police. And there are important exceptions to the prohibitions on access to a bank customer's records by federal agents; among them are the following.[4]

1.   "Emergency access" is permitted without formal process if a federal-agency official of supervisory rank determines that immediate access is necessary because of the imminent danger of physical injury to any person or serious property damage or of flight to avoid prosecution. If emergency access is obtained, the agency must file a sworn explanatory statement with a federal district court within five days and must thereafter notify the bank customer that his records have been obtained.

2.   Foreign-intelligence and counterintelligence agents and Secret Service agents performing protective functions (e.g., guarding the president) are permitted to obtain bank records merely by request. In such instances, the bank releasing the customer's records to the federal agent is forbidden to disclose to anyone the fact that the records were sought or obtained.

3.   Such supervisory and regulatory agencies as the Fed-

eral Deposit Insurance Corporation, the Federal Reserve Board, the Securities and Exchange Commission, and analogous state banking and securities agencies are permitted to examine bank records in accordance with existing statutes that define their functions. The Secretary of the Treasury is permitted to examine bank records in accordance with the Bank Secrecy Act, its interpretive regulations, and the Foreign Transactions Reporting Act. Access by Internal Revenue Service agents is governed by the Internal Revenue Code.

4.   When a customer is under consideration for a federal loan, loan guarantee, or loan insurance program, the appropriate agency may examine his or her bank records without formal legal process.

5.   Normal procedures for obtaining records under the US Code and Federal Rules of Civil and Criminal Procedure apply when the records are sought in the course of litigation to which the government is a party.

6.   When disclosure of bank records to federal agencies are required by any other federal law or regulation, the Right to Financial Privacy Act does not override such requirements.

In addition to the restrictions placed upon the powers of federal agencies to obtain records, the RFPA does place certain obligations upon banks to protect the rights of their customers. A bank is not permitted to release a customer's records to a federal agency except in accordance with the requirements of the statute. However, the bank is permitted to notify a federal agent of the fact that it has in its possession information that may be relevant to a possible violation of a law or regulation.[5] Then, to obtain that information, the agency has to comply with the applicable procedures required by the statute.

How does a bank customer authorize disclosures of his records under the Right to Financial Privacy Act?

An authorization must be written, signed, dated, and presented to both the bank and the federal agency that will receive the records. No authorization is valid for more than three months, and it may be revoked at any time during those three months. The authorization must specify which records are to be disclosed and the purposes for which the government will use them. At the time of authorization, the bank must notify its customer of his or her rights under the RFPA. No financial institution may require a customer's authorization as a condition of doing business.[6]

How are federal government agencies limited in the purposes for which they may seek a person's bank records by a subpoena, summons, warrant, or formal written request?

To obtain bank records pursuant to an administrative subpoena or summons, a court order, or a formal written request, the agency need only have "reason to believe that the records sought are relevant to a legitimate law enforcement inquiry." To obtain bank records pursuant to a search warrant, the agency must meet a higher standard of "probable cause" to believe that an offense has been or is about to be committed and that the bank records will yield pertinent evidence.[7] The higher standard required for a search warrant is complemented by the agency's freedom to obtain the records without delay or prior notification to the bank customer.

How does the customer know that his bank records are being sought or have been obtained by a federal agency?

If the agency seeks access to the records by an administrative subpoena or summons, a court order, or a formal written request, the agency must serve or mail a copy to the customer at his last known address; this must be done on or before the date when it is served upon the bank. At the same time, the agency must give the customer a written explanation of (1) the nature of the law-enforcement inquiry to which the records are believed relevant and (2) the Right to Financial Privacy Act's provisions whereby a customer may challenge the agency's attempt to obtain the records. The agency may not actually obtain the records from the bank until ten days after notice has been served to the customer or fourteen days after it has been mailed. If the agency seeks access with a search warrant, it may notify the customer at any time within ninety days after the warrant is served upon the bank. Once a warrant has been served, the bank must release the records immediately. However, the act also allows agencies to delay notice to the customer, for successive periods of ninety days, by authorization of a federal district court. The agency must satisfy the court that its law-enforcement investigation is within the agency's lawful jurisdiction, that the records are relevant, and that immediate notice to the customer might result in one of the following:

1. Danger to the life or physical safety of any person;
2. Flight from prosecution;
3. Destruction of or tampering with evidence;
4. Intimidation of potential witnesses; or
5. Serious jeopardy to the investigation or undue delay of a trial or official proceeding.

These generous conditions could in practice be applied to justify an indefinite delay of notification to a bank customer simply because an agency does not wish to be bothered by a customer's challenge to its request for access. After a delay granted by the court expires, the agency must serve or mail the records to the customer "as soon as practicable" thereafter. However, if the records are obtained by foreign-intelligence or Secret Service agents, the customer it is investigating is informed.[8]

If records are sought with a customer's own authorization, the bank must keep an accounting of all disclosures it makes under the authorization and make that accounting available to the customer on request—unless an agency obtains a court order permitting delay of such notification.[9]

Another method of learning whether a federal agency may have obtained information from one's bank records is to use the access provisions of the Freedom of Information Act to examine the records maintained by a federal agency. Although certain federal-agency investigative records cannot be obtained under the FOIA, sufficient information might be accessible to suggest that the agency had, in fact, examined bank records.

Assuming that the customer does receive prior notice, what can the customer do if he or she wishes to challenge the pursuit of access to his or her records?

A customer may challenge in court the agency's attempt to obtain his bank records. To do so, he or she must state to the court the reasons for believing that the records are *not* relevant to the law-enforcement inquiry cited by the government (thus, perhaps, being forced to reveal some of the very information he is trying to protect) or that the government has not substantially complied with the requirements of the act. The court must then decide whether the government's investigation is legitimate, whether the records sought are relevant, and whether the agency has substantially complied with all required procedures. On this basis, the court will either grant or deny the agency's request. In a highly controversial provision, the act limits the customer's challenge to these stated procedures, thus appearing to prevent any attempt to mount a challenge on other statutory grounds or even on constitutional grounds.[10]

The agency's notification to the customer will state that it is not necessary to have an attorney in order to challenge the agency's action in court. But it is not wise to attempt such a potentially complex procedure without expert advice; those who receive notice that their bank records are being sought and wish to resist should consult an attorney if possible.

Once a federal agency has obtained a customer's records, may it pass them on to other agencies?

Yes, if the agency certifies in writing that the transfer is being made because it believes that the records are relevant to a legitimate law-enforcement inquiry within the jurisdiction of the receiving agency. Notice of such a transfer must be given to the customer within fourteen days, unless the agency obtains a court order permitting delay of notification.[11]

Has there been much litigation under the RFPA?

No, mainly because the law has forced agencies to be more careful about seeking financial records, and the law requires customers trying to block government access to show why their files are not "relevant" to an investigation—a tough standard to meet. The most significant case to date involved the army's failure to follow the law while obtaining the American Express billing records of Lieutenant Colonel Duncan who worked on intelligence operations. The army was conducting an audit of the secret military operation for which he was responsible and maintained that a subpoena or court order might jeopardize the "integrity" of the undercover operation. The army convinced American Express to turn over the files without notifying Colonel Duncan or his wife. A federal appeals court said this was a violation of the RFPA, stating that Duncan and his wife met the act's definition of customer and that the audit exception did not apply because it was the army, and not the Duncans, who requested the audit. The appeals panel said the couple was entitled to damages and ordered the lower court to come up with an appropriate figure.[12]

In 1981, the Securities and Exchange Commission overlooked its responsibilities and failed to notify Nelson and Bunker Hunt that it was seeking their bank records for a probe into speculation in the silver market. A federal judge scolded the SEC for negligence of financial privacy requirements, but the commission eventually obtained the Hunt's files anyway.[13]

According to an oversight report, customers challenged federal agency requests for their bank files only seventy-four times between 1979 and 1985.[14] Customer challenges are ordinarily rejected, and the only other successful challenge came in Texas in response to a Social Security Administration bid for a person's financial file.[15]

Are there laws protecting bank customers against disclosure of their records to state authorities?

Yes. A few states have enacted bank privacy statutes that require a state or local government agency to obtain bank records only by formal legal process.[16] A number of these are more stringent than the federal statute is with respect to federal agencies.

Some state supreme courts have declared that financial records are protected from informal government access by state constitutions. The Colorado Supreme Court recognized that the US Supreme Court's decision in *U.S. v. Miller* precluded Fourth Amendment protection of bank records but stated that *Miller* did not prevent the recognition of an independent right to protection under the Colorado Constitution.[17] The court applied the expectation of privacy test derived from the Warren Court's *Katz v. U.S.*[18] and inquired "whether the bank depositor has a reasonable expectation of privacy in the bank records of his financial transactions." The court concluded that the bank depositor did have such an expectation of privacy and thus was entitled to protection by the Colorado Constitution. Similarly, courts in California,[19] Illinois,[20] and Pennsylvania[21] have protected expectations of privacy in bank records, thus differing with *U.S. v. Miller*. On the other hand, many state courts have followed *Miller*, limiting state constitutional protection for privacy of bank records. These include Georgia, Indiana, New York, North Carolina, Washington State, and Wyoming.[22] Furthermore, in many states, where neither statutes nor constitutional provisions restrict access, state and local police and other authorities can legally obtain a customer's bank records merely by an informal unwritten request to the bank. It is then left entirely to the discretion of the bank whether to comply.

Bank policies on these matters vary widely. Some will respond only to formal legal process, others to a written request on the agency's official stationery. Some allow their branches a degree of discretion so that particular branch managers or security chiefs may even comply with oral requests from government officials. Banks also vary on the question of prior notification to the customer. Some adhere to strict policies in this regard and take upon themselves the responsibility for informing the customer that his records have been subpoenaed. In other banks the matter is handled on a case-by-case basis by their legal counsel, who may be persuaded in particular circumstances to honor an agency's request that a customer not be notified. What this means to bank customers is simply that the privacy of records is at the mercy of their banker. That being so, it is wise to ask one's bank for a written statement of its policies with regard to government demands for customer records.

May banks release information from a customer's records to a third party that is not a government agency?

Yes. Ordinary business practice governs many situations in which a private party having some business or financial relationship with a customer (such as a creditor) may obtain information about him from his bank. Often the customer is informed that this will be necessary and is asked to give consent. But sometimes banks will reveal information about a customer, without consent, to independent check-guarantee or check-verification services, to collection agencies, to credit-reporting agencies and credit bureaus, or to individual credit grantors. Banks follow individual policies as to how much and what kinds of information they will reveal in each of these circumstances and as to any notice, before or after the fact, to the customer.

There is a growing common-law doctrine of the duty of confidentiality that banks owe their customers, developed through a series of state court decisions,[23] which suggests that banks have a legal obligation not to disclose information about their customers to private third parties. The thrust of these decisions is that customers may be able to protect themselves from certain exceptional disclosure to private third parties, especially when the disclosures might cause some tangible (usually financial) harm to the customer. However, they would not apply to disclosures made in the course of ordinary business practice.

How does the Bank Secrecy Act affect the confidentiality of bank records?

The Bank Secrecy Act of 1970[24] places legal obligations upon banks to maintain certain records of customers' transactions for specific periods and to report certain of those transactions to the federal government. The law requires the US Treasury Department to write detailed regulations interpreting the act.[25] The act's original purpose was to force US citizens to disclose their foreign accounts and foreign currency transactions in order to prevent circumvention of currency and tax laws. Banks are required, for example, to maintain records of instructions from their customers concerning the transmission of funds, currency, and credit out of the country in amounts over $10,000, and travelers must report the transportation into or out of the US of currency in amounts over $10,000.

Of greater concern to the ordinary bank customer are the provisions that banks must keep, for five years, a microfilmed copy of the front and back of every check over $100, all account statements, all signature-authority documents, and all records necessary to reconstruct a checking account and furnish an audit trail for transactions over $100. The act and regulations require brokers and banks to obtain the customer's Social Security number or other taxpayer identification number for trading and deposit accounts and require banks to report to the Internal Revenue Service any "unusual" domestic currency transactions of more than $2,500.

The practical result of these and other provisions of the act and its regulations is that every record of every transaction by every customer is preserved and potentially available for government examination. (The $100 cut-off figure for the check-recording requirement is meaningless, because the banks find it much too expensive to sort out checks for amounts under $100. Therefore, microfilms are taken of all checks, front and back, and kept for five years.)

If, as the highest California state court once observed, a person's bank records are the mirror of his life, "a virtual current biography,"[26] the implementation of the Bank Secrecy Act produces a complete, permanent image of the customer's personal, private life. And because, according to the Supreme Court, a person has no constitutional expectation of privacy in bank records, that image is potentially accessible to government officials without the person's consent, in some cases even without knowledge.

Despite the scope of the act and of the Treasury Department regulations and despite their clear implications for the right of financial privacy, in 1974 the Supreme Court upheld the constitutionality of the act against a challenge based on the First Amendment right of privacy of association, the Fourth Amendment right to freedom from unreasonable search and seizure, and the Fifth Amendment privilege against self-incrimination.[27] Although Congress subsequently enacted the Right to Financial Privacy Act of 1978 to provide some statutory protection for bank records, this Supreme Court decision on the Bank Secrecy Act and the Court's 1976 ruling mentioned earlier place the bank customer in a very vulnerable position with respect to any reasonable expectation that bank records will be protected from access by government officials.

What laws protect the confidentiality of federal tax records?

Under the Tax Reform Act of 1976, amending the Internal Revenue Code,[28] federal tax returns and other personal information submitted to or collected by the Internal Revenue Service may not be revealed to anyone outside the IRS without the individual's authorization, except for specifically enumerated purposes. The major exceptions to the confidentiality provisions of the Tax Reform Act, permitting disclosure of a taxpayer's return or return information without his authorization, are as follows:

1.   To state tax officials, upon the written request of the head of a state tax agency or commission.

2.   To persons having a "material interest." Such persons might include trustees, spouses, business partners, guardians of a legally incompetent taxpayer, or receivers of the property of a bankrupt taxpayer.

3.   To certain committees of the Congress. If a particular taxpayer is or could be identified in the returns disclosed, the congressional committee may receive them only while sitting in closed session, unless the taxpayer consents in writing to disclosure in open session.

4.   To the president and certain White House officials designated by the president. This may be done only upon the president's written request, specifying the information sought and the reasons for the request. All such requests must be reported to the Joint Congressional Committee on Taxation. The act contains special provisions allowing presidential scrutiny of tax information concerning candidates for appointment to certain federal executive or judicial positions.

5.   To employees of the Treasury Department and the Department of Justice for purposes of enforcing the tax laws. For example, returns or return information may be released to a US attorney in contemplation of a proceeding before a federal grand jury or federal or state court concerning a violation of the tax laws. Under some circumstances, a taxpayer's return could be disclosed pursuant to this provision even if that particular taxpayer is not himself the target of the investigation or prosecution.

6.   To attorneys for use in screening prospective jurors in a tax case. This highly controversial provision, which was

opposed by the Privacy Protection Study Commission,[29] permits both government and defense attorneys to ask IRS whether a prospective juror has been the subject of an IRS audit or investigation. The purported reason for such disclosures is to weed out jurors who may harbor personal resentments against the IRS, but the Privacy Commission called the value of such information "marginal" and pointed out that the same information can be obtained by directly questioning of the prospective juror in court.

7.   To another federal agency for purposes of administering federal laws other than the tax laws. In a non-tax criminal investigation, a taxpayer's return or return information may be disclosed by order of a federal district court judge. The judge must determine that there is reasonable cause to believe that a specific criminal act has been committed, that the return contains evidence related to the crime, and that the same evidence could not reasonably be obtained from some other source. The taxpayer need not be informed of the judicial proceeding by which the release of his tax records is authorized and so has no opportunity to contest the disclosure. Additionally, the IRS may disclose to other federal agencies for use in non-tax criminal investigations certain information in its possession that comes from a source other than the taxpayer's return and may make disclosures of this kind without court order. Such other sources might be bank or credit card records previously obtained by the IRS, or an informant.

8.   To certain other agencies for specified purposes, such as the administration of the Social Security and Railroad Retirement Acts, the location of missing parents under child-support enforcement programs, and the notification through the press of persons to whom IRS owes refunds.

Federal and state officials (including former officials) who make disclosures of taxpayer information not authorized by this statute can be punished by imprisonment of up to five years and a fine of up to $5000. In addition, the aggrieved taxpayer may bring a civil action to recover actual damages against officials who knowingly or negligently make an unauthorized disclosure and for punitive damages in addition if the official acted willfully or with gross negligence.[30]

Does the IRS receive financial data from other federal agencies?

Yes. Pursuant to the Deficit Reduction Act of 1984, the IRS created the IRS Debtor Master file. The database was created using information from the records of a number of federal agencies and was to aid in the administering of tax refunds to collect on delinquent federal debts, such as student loans.

What about state tax records?

Most states have statutes protecting the confidentiality of information submitted to or gathered by state tax authorities. These vary widely in the safeguards they provide and in the disclosures they permit. The Tax Reform Act of 1976 requires state tax authorities to establish administrative safeguards for the confidentiality of information they receive from the IRS. If a state requires a taxpayer to submit a copy of his federal tax return along with his state return, the act provides that the state must have statutory, not merely administrative, safeguards for the confidentiality of tax information.[31] In general, protection against the unauthorized disclosure of either federal or state tax information by state authorities is weaker and harder to enforce than that applicable to the IRS itself.

May a person have access to his or her tax records?

Yes. Rights of access to and correction of one's own tax records (including not only returns but also information collected by the tax agency from other sources) are governed by the federal Privacy Act and Freedom of Information Act, in the case of IRS records, and by analogous state privacy statutes where these have been enacted. These statutes can also be used to determine what disclosures of personal information have been made by tax agencies to other agencies or persons. In states that do not have privacy acts, a state freedom-of-information law can often be used to obtain access to one's own state tax records.

If a person believes that his or her bank or tax records have been disclosed illegally, what should he or she do?

Consult a lawyer. The statutes and regulations concerning financial privacy are complex and vary widely from state to state. Expert legal advice is necessary to determine whether a violation of law has occurred and what remedies might be available.

NOTES

1. *U.S. v. Miller*, 425 U.S. 435 (1976).
2. 31 U.S.C. § 1051.
3. 12 U.S.C. § 3401 *et seq*.
4. *Id*. at 3413, 3414.
5. *Id*. at 3403.
6. *Id*. at 3404.
7. *Id*. at 3404.
8. *Id*. at 3405–8.
9. *Id*. at 3409 and 3414(a)(3).
10. *Id*. at 3410.
11. *Id*. at 3412.
12. *Duncan v. Belcher and American Express* 813 F.2d 1335 (4th Cir. 1987).
13. *SEC v. Hunt* 520 F. Supp. 580 (N.D. Tex. 1981).
14. Administrative Office of the U.S. Courts, *Report on Applications for Delays of Notice and Customer Challenges Under Provisions of Right to Financial Privacy Act of 1978*, Calendar Year 1985.
15. *See Kauffman v. Dep't. of Army*, No. 83-SJ-03 (W.D. Mo.; Aug. 5, 1983); *Granstrom v. SEC*, 532 F. Supp. 1023 (S.D.N.Y. 1982); *Hancock v. Marshall*, 86 F.R.D. 209 (D.D.C. 1980); *McGloshen v. Dept. of Agriculture*, 480 F. Supp. 247 (W.D. Ky. 1979).
16. *See* Or. Rev. Stat. §§ 192.550–595; Md. Ann. Code art. 11, § 224 *et seq*.; Alaska Stat. § 06.05.175; Ill. Rev. Stat. ch. 16 1/2, para. 48.1; Cal. Gov't. Code, § 7460 *et seq*.
17. *Charnes v. DiGiacomo*, 612 P.2d 1117 (D. Colo. 1980).
18. 389 U.S. 347 (1967).
19. *Valley Bank of Nevada v. Sup. Ct. of San Joaquin City*, 542 P.2d 977 (Cal. 1975).
20. *People v. Jackson*, 452 N.E. 2d 85 (Ill. App. Ct. 1983).
21. *Commonwealth v. DeJohn*, 403 A.2d 1283 (Pa. 1979).
22. There are states that have adhered to *U.S. v. Miller* or have otherwise denied a person rights of privacy in his bank records at the state level. *See, e.g., Adams v. Trust Co. Bank*, 244 S.E.2d 651 (Ga. Ct. App. 1978) (depositor has no privacy interest in copies of his bank records); *Cox v. State*, 392 N.E.2d 496 (Ind. Ct. App. 1976) (no

privacy interest in bank records); *People v. Cappelta*, 392 N.Y.S.2d 996 (N.Y. App. Div. 1977) (search and seizure of bank records not unlawful as there is no Fourth Amendment interest in bank records), *aff'd*, 399 N.Y.S.2d 638 (N.Y. 1977); *State v. Sheetz*, 265 S.E.2d 914 (N.C. Ct. App. 1980) (bank customer cannot contest sheriff department's examination of his bank records); *State v. Union State Bank*, 267 N.W. 2d 777 (N.D. 1978) (no privacy interest in bank records as they are the property of the bank); *Peters v. Sjoholm*, 604 P.2d 527 (Wash. Ct. App. 1979), *aff'd*, 631 P.2d 937 (Wash. 1981) (no privacy interest in bank records under state or federal constitutions), *cert. denied*, 455 U.S. 914 (1982); *Fitzgerald v. State*, 599 P.2d 572 (Wyo. 1979) (person has no expectation of privacy in bank records even where policy obtained records from bank voluntarily).

23. *See* Privacy Protection Study Commission, *Personal Privacy in an Information Society* (U.S. Government Printing Office, July 1977), Appendix I, Privacy Law in the States 25–27.
24. 31 U.S.C. 1051 *et seq*.
25. These are published at 31 C.F.R. § 103.
26. *Burrows v. Super. Court*, 13 Cal. 3d 238 (1974).
27. *California Bankers Ass'n v. Schultz*, 416 U.S. 21 (1974).
28. Pub. L. No. 94-455, § 1202, amending 26 U.S.C. § 6103.
29. Privacy Protection Study Commission, *Personal Privacy in an Information Society*, 545.
30. 26 U.S.C. § 7217.
31. 26 U.S.C. § 6103(p).

XII

Medical and Insurance Records

Is there a basis for doctor-patient confidentiality?
Yes. It has its roots in the oath for physicians put forth by Hippocrates more than two thousand years ago. The Hippocratic oath states "All that may come to my knowledge in the exercise of my profession or outside of my profession or in daily commerce with man which ought not to be spread abroad, I will keep secret and never reveal." Traditionally, people who had access to health care were treated by their own physicians, many of whom adhered to the Hippocratic oath and, as sole custodians of their patients' medical information, protected its confidentiality. But the health care system has undergone a dramatic transformation. Doctors still treat patients, but an entire bureaucracy has arisen to facilitate financing and payment of health care. Many people have health insurance through their employers. Others are covered directly by insurers. Still others receive health benefits from federal, state, or local governments. All of these third party payers (employers, insurers, and governments) and providers (doctors, hospitals, HMOs, clinics, etc.) need access to medical information in order to administer health coverage and verify payments.

More than forty states have statutes that protect the confidentiality of communications between physician (or psychiatrist) and patient—the doctor-patient privilege. But these statutes merely prevent the doctor from being forced to testify about the patient's communications or reveal the patient's records in a court of law without the patient's consent. They have no application to the enormous number of situations in which a physician is permitted or compelled, by law, regulation, or long-established practice, to reveal information about the patient to outside parties. Even under doctor-patient privilege laws, doctors may be required to testify about a patient or reveal a patient's records. In a criminal case, medical testimony may be introduced by the prosecution or the defense. In a civil case—such as a negligence or malpractice suit, a divorce or custody suit, or a commitment proceeding—the medical history and condition of the principals may be the primary questions at issue.[1] In any of these situations, a patient's physician may be required by the court to describe his medical history and even produce his records.

A further restriction upon the reach of privilege statutes is that they apply only in cases governed by state law. The Federal Rules of Evidence, which govern practice in federal courts, provide only a psychotherapist-patient privilege, not a general doctor-patient privilege. Under the Federal Rules, communications between physician and patient may be revealed at the discretion of the court, guided in its judgment by "the principles of the common law as they may be interpreted by the courts of the United States in the light of reason and experience." Where state law is applicable to a case, the privilege is determined "in accordance with the state law."[2]

Though the words "doctor-patient privilege" are often used rhetorically to describe the principle of confidentiality that is popularly attributed to the relationship between doctor and patient, the privilege is in reality a narrowly drawn rule of evidence, not even recognized in the common law (as is, for example, the attorney-client privilege), but available only where it is specifically provided by statute.

What do today's medical records contain?

There is a wide variety of data. The common categories are past medical history, social history, which concerns lifestyle matters such as smoking, sexual practices, exercise and diet, family history (concerning diseases common to the patient's family), review of systems (including health details that might not be related to the problem of the day), and objective information (including data from lab tests, X-rays, or other check up procedures). Hospital records typically contain a physician's order sheet, daily nursing care sheet, graphic record (which charts temperature, blood pressure, and other measurements), and a pathology report which details the results of operations.

To whom do doctors and hospitals commonly reveal patients' records?

The following is a partial list, noting only the most common recipients of information and records.

Insurance companies. Both to establish an applicant's eligibility for health, life, and disability policies and to process claims under such policies, insurance companies require extensive medical information from the patient's physicians and psychiatrists and from his hospital records. So much medical information is collected by insurance companies, in fact, that the industry maintains its own giant medical databank, called the Medical Information Bureau.

Government service payers. The government agencies that finance and administer Medicare, Medicaid, Social Security disability, and workmen's compensation programs all require the submission of patient treatment records as a prerequisite for authorizing payments. State and federal agencies that administer special services, such as treatment for drug addiction and alcoholism, mental health problems, and physical handicaps, frequently require access to or information from the patient's records.

Welfare agencies. The many government agencies involved in the administration of welfare and social service programs often require detailed information about their clients' medical problems and treatment.

Professional accrediting agencies and review boards. Public and private agencies use patient records to evaluate the quality of professional services provided by doctors and health-care facilities.

Researchers. Many medical research projects use patient records. Usually, the information can be provided to researchers in aggregate statistical form, but some projects utilize individual, identifiable patient records.

Employers. Applicants for employment are often asked to fill out extensive medical questionnaires and in addition to give prospective employers authorization to see their physician and hospital records. Applicants and current employees may be required to undergo examinations by company doctors. Employers also obtain diagnostic and treatment information about their employees through claims submitted under company [provided] insurance plans.

Credit-reporting agencies. Private credit-reporting agencies compile medical histories and claims investigations for employers and insurance companies, frequently containing information taken directly from physician and hospital records.

Public-health and law-enforcement agencies.   Many state laws require hospitals, physicians, and other health-care providers to report certain kinds of diseases, injuries, and treatments to a public health department or even directly to the police. These may include venereal disease, drug abuse, suspected incidents of child abuse, gunshot wounds, many contagious and epidemic diseases such as typhoid and scarlet fever, abortions, and prescriptions for certain kinds of drugs. Government agencies, such as the National Institute for Occupational Safety and Health, generally can obtain access to employees' health records to use in studies of environmental and occupational hazards. Police departments can gain access to medical records in the course of criminal investigations.

Licensing agencies.   State occupational licensing requirements usually include the submission of medical and psychiatric records.

Institutions.   When medical services are provided in an institutional setting, such as a school or college, prison, or the armed services, nonmedical personnel within the institution may have access to a patient's records.

Databanks.   As a routine adjunct to many of the uses of medical records just described, computerized registries or databanks of particular kinds of patients are maintained by a wide variety of public and private agencies, from state and local governments to insurance companies and national charities. There are, for example, registries of patients receiving certain prescription drugs, abortion patients, cancer patients, handicapped persons, psychiatric patients, drug addicts, and clients of state-financed medical services. Such patients are seldom even aware that these databanks exist.

In 1977 the Supreme Court rejected a privacy challenge to a New York law creating a state-operated index containing the names of all patients in the state for whom certain "dangerous legitimate drugs" were prescribed. The Court said that it upheld the law because it incorporated safeguards for notice, fairness, security, and confidentiality, and because no tangible harm was demonstrated.[3]

What is the Medical Information Bureau?

The Medical Information Bureau (MIB) is the world's largest electronic network of health data. Created by insurance industry physicians and medical directors as a loose-knit manual system in 1902, the MIB has mushroomed into a mammoth "credit bureau" for health data designed to prevent fraud by life and health applicants who fail to give complete or accurate medical histories. Over 750 life insurance companies participate in the on-line exchange of medical data with the MIB. Health conditions are reported by using one or more of about 210 codes. Conditions most commonly reported include height and weight, blood pressure, EKG readings, and X-rays, "but only if significant to the underwriting evaluation," according to the MIB's fact sheet.

Nonmedical information relating to such issues as reckless driving, hazardous sports, and aviation activity is covered by five additional codes.

What rights do patients have in relation to the MIB?

Few legal rights, except under scattered state laws. However in 1971, the MIB adopted many of the fair information practices that the Privacy Protection Study Commission recommended for all industries five years later. These include the right to obtain a copy of one's own records and correct inaccurate data. Disclosure is restricted as well. Member companies can obtain a person's file only after he or she has signed a written authorization in connection with a pending application for coverage. Reports are not supposed to be released to nonmember companies, credit or consumer reporting agencies, or government agencies lacking a court order.

Insurers are not permitted to make an underwriting decision on the basis of data provided by the MIB. Instead MIB is meant to be an alert system, in which insurers must independently corroborate data they get. Insurers also are required to submit data on applicants and customers to the MIB.[4] MIB rules require that insurers provide applicants with a written notice of data exchange practices and consumer access rights. According to MIB, seven thousand people each year request access to their files, of which two hundred seek corrections.[5]

Are there plans for additional nationwide, health-related data banks?

Yes. As this book went to press in 1989, the US Department

of Health and Human Services (HHS) is in the process of creating a central computer to track prescription purchases by 32 million Medicare beneficiaries. The plan calls for the government to finance and install 52,000 computer terminals in pharmacies across the nation. It also calls for different insurance carriers to be designated as regional data clearinghouses in order to keep track of payments to physicians. The system reportedly will cost $12 million and is designed to cut fraud and waste in federally underwritten prescription purchases. But key members of Congress, the American Civil Liberties Union, and pharmacologists are expressing concern about the implications for privacy due to the unprecedented concentration by the government of sensitive prescription data without adequate legal and administrative safeguards.[6] A separate plan, announced by the HHS in November 1988, is the creation of a national databank on health care treatment of 32 million elderly and disabled people who participate in the Medicare program. The proposal entails trilateral, electronic hookups between the federal government, private insurers and organizations that make or monitor Medicare payments, and Professional Review Organizations (PROs). The goal of the system is to provide the first comprehensive database enabling medical providers to pinpoint which treatments are most effective for various illnesses. Theoretically, it will allow the Health Care Financing Administration (HCFA) to identify ineffective treatments and adopt new nonpayment policies for them. The system, named the National Health Care Information Resource Center, is expected to be operational by the end of 1990 at a cost of $10 to $20 million. William L. Roper, head of the HCFA acknowledged that the system will centralize unprecedented amounts of sensitive medical data at the federal level and pledged "maximum regard" for the privacy of Medicare patients.[7]

Can patients prevent doctors and hospitals from disclosing their records?

For all practical purposes, no. In the case of insurance companies and government agencies that reimburse medical services, the patient routinely authorizes the release of his records in a blanket waiver or general consent, which must be signed as a condition of receiving a policy or reimbursement on a claim. Except in California,[8] the waiver does not specify the particular records to be sought or the particular doctors and hospitals to be contacted, nor does it ordinarily provide an expiration date beyond which the consent is invalid. In fact some waivers cover not only the signatory but also all other family members. Having signed a waiver, the patient has little leverage to resist the company's or government's demands for his records. Occasionally, a particularly alert doctor or hospital records administrator will balk at what is felt to be an excessive demand, such as for the complete patient record rather than information directly pertinent to a claim, or for the details of a psychiatric diagnosis and prognosis. But here the initiative for protecting a patient's privacy lies with the practitioner or hospital. There is little that the patient can do.

It is extremely difficult for a job applicant to resist an employer's demand for medical information, either on a questionnaire or through access to his doctor and hospital records. In most instances, the demand is an implied requirement for consideration of the person's application. There has been little litigation of this issue. In one successful legal challenge to an intrusive preemployment medical inquiry on privacy grounds, a county government was forced to drop questions about applicants' emotional problems, mental health treatment, use of drugs and alcohol, and "female disorders," to withdraw its blanket release form that forced applicants to authorize county access to all of their medical records, and to pay money damages to an applicant who lost a job because she refused to answer questions she considered offensive.[9]

Most waivers on employment applications, like those on insurance policies, are blanket consents, permitting the employer (or a credit-reporting agency on the employer's behalf) to have access to all of the applicant's medical records. Occasionally, applicants manage at least to limit the effective date of the consent so that it cannot be reused later. If the employer is going to get medical information through an investigation made by a credit-reporting agency, the applicant might attempt to use his statutory right to be told the "nature and scope" of the investigation[10] as an opportunity to receive a more specific description of the records to be obtained and even to refine the wording of the consent form he must sign.

When an applicant or employee is to be examined by a
company physician, it is a good idea to ascertain ahead of time
what kinds of information the physician will pass along to the
employer. Unless explicit assurances of complete confidentiality are given, the patient should assume that some disclosures will be made to the employer—who is of course the
physician's employer too.

Medical records are generally made available for research,
accrediting, and professional review purposes without the
patient's knowledge. The laws, regulations, and traditional
professional practices governing these functions do not ordinarily include provisions for either notification or consent.[11]
Mandatory public reporting laws, of course, obviate a need
for patient consent.

Law-enforcement officers are often able to obtain information from doctors and hospitals informally, simply by announcing that a police investigation is involved. Only the
most resolute practitioner or hospital administrator is likely
to demand a search warrant or court order before turning over
patient records. Again it is in the hands of the doctor or
hospital, not the patient, to decide whether to resist such a
demand.

In general, therefore, patients have little opportunity to
prevent disclosures of information from their own medical
records. The widespread use of the blanket consent form,
together with the traditional presumption that medical records "belong" to doctors and hospitals rather than to the
individuals whom they describe, conspire to give patients
very little direct control over the privacy of their records. On
one occasion the US government went too far. Seeking to
force health care providers to give maximum care to all
newborns, the HHS in 1983 adopted so-called "Baby Doe"
regulations under federal handicap laws, which gave the
department twenty-four-hour access to hospital records
related to the treatment of handicapped infants who may have
been denied treatment. But a federal judge voided the rules
for being arbitrary and capricious, explaining that spurious
investigation involving immediate inspection of hospital
records would have a disruptive effect and interfere with
proper treatment.[12]

In a different kind of case, the Florida Supreme Court ruled in 1987 that an AIDS victim could not force a blood donor bank to disclose the names and addresses of all of its blood donors. The court said that the privacy interests of blood donors and society's interest in maintaining strong volunteer blood donation system outweighed the victim's interest, which could be protected under present discovery rules that would allow for verification that none of the blood donors had AIDS while still preserving confidentiality.[13]

Aren't there laws restricting disclosures of information by doctors and hospitals?

Yes, but most are riddled with exemptions, and where these specific exemptions do not apply, the laws can easily be circumvented by the routine use of patient waivers. More than thirty states have statutes restricting access to physician and hospital records. Some have a special statute applying to medical or psychiatric records; others simply list medical records as an exempted category in state freedom of information laws. Some deal only with medical records in public hospitals and clinics; some apply to both the public and private sectors. But all permit a wide range of disclosures without patient consent for research, audit, accrediting, investigative, judicial, emergency, and public health reporting purposes, and of course permit disclosure with patient consent to insurers, employers, and other interested persons. In some statutes, an attempt has been made to refine the procedures necessary to obtain patient consent. In a 1977 Oregon law, for example, patient consent to disclosures of medical records held by public hospitals and other public health care providers must name the agency in which the records are being held, the person or organization to whom disclosure is to be made, the purpose of the disclosure, and the nature and extent of the information to be disclosed. It must be signed and dated by the patient and specify a date or condition of expiration. It may be revoked at any time, even before the stated expiration date.[14] Still, a person whose insurance company or prospective employer demands that he execute such a consent presumably has no realistic choice but to do so.

In addition to state laws that protect the confidentiality of medical records specifically, there are other privacy statutes that can be applied to physician and hospital records. The Privacy Act of 1974, for example, restricts disclosures of medical records held by federal hospitals, the Indian Health Service, the Public Health Service, and other federal health-care facilities.[15] Similarly state privacy laws, where they exist, do the same for medical records in clinics, hospitals, and treatment programs run by state and local government agencies. But it must be remembered that the federal act and most of its state analogs provide for disclosures to law enforcement agencies, and for "routine uses," which can be administratively interpreted to encompass many interagency and outside disclosures for payment, review, research, public health reporting, auditing, and investigative purposes. Also, patient waivers can be coerced even under privacy statutes, in that the patient has no effective opportunity to refuse if he wants treatment or reimbursement for treatment. The Family Educational Rights and Privacy Act, dealing with student records, limits the disclosures that school and college medical personnel may make to other persons within or outside the school community without the student's authorization. However, the "health and safety" emergency exceptions to the disclosure prohibitions of both the Family Educational Rights and Privacy Act and the federal Privacy Act of 1974, as well as analogous state statutes, would frequently apply to disclosures of medical and psychiatric information.[16]

Many federal and state health care programs are governed by formal regulations that are supposed to prevent disclosures of patient records. Once again, these are usually written to allow many routine disclosures to other government agencies that have some involvement with the patient—welfare departments are a common example—as well as for law-enforcement and research purposes and for entry into various governmental medical databanks, such as abortion, addict, or client service registries. Disclosures that cannot be accomplished within the regulations can usually be authorized by obtaining the patient's signature on a consent form presented in such a way that the patient has no real choice but to sign.

There is no way to reduce to simple terms the confused tangle of laws and regulations dealing with the privacy of physician and hospital records. A particular patient's records may be subject to any number of overlapping or even conflict-

ing sets of restrictions. But two generalizations—both dis-
couraging—can be made. First, many disclosures from doctor
and hospital records to third parties can be made under the
terms of existing statutes and regulations, without need for
patient consent or even notification. The patient may not be
able to prevent these disclosures but should at least try to find
out what they are. It is worth taking the time to discuss with
one's doctor under what conditions, and for what purposes, he
or she would release information to third parties without
prior patient authorization. It is also well worth the extra
effort necessary to ask the same questions of administrative
personnel in the hospitals and clinics where one has received
treatment. Such questioning does more than inform the
patient; it also puts doctors and hospitals on notice that
patients are concerned about their privacy and thus alerts
them to be more careful in making disclosures to outsiders.
The second generalization is that patient "consent" to a
disclosure is often an empty ritual. Such consent is usually
demanded in circumstances leaving the patient little choice
but to grant it. If there is a choice, patients would do well to
ask for specific information before deciding whether to sign:
what records will be released, to whom, for what purposes,
what will happen to the records when the purpose is fulfilled,
who will have access to them, and for how long. Whenever
possible, the consent form should be reworded to reflect all
these conditions.

Are there special legal protections for "sensitive" medical records, such as psychiatric or drug abuse treatment records?

Yes, some. There is, in both law and practice, a growing
recognition that many patients will not seek certain kinds of
treatment—for drug and alcohol addiction, venereal disease,
mental and emotional problems, abortion, even contraceptive services—if they have to fear the stigma of disclosure. As
noted earlier, many states have statutes granting a privilege to
communications between psychiatrists and patients or protecting the confidentiality of mental patients' records, and the
Federal Rules of Evidence recognize a psychiatrist-patient
privilege. Also as noted earlier, these legislative and judicial
safeguards are seriously flawed.

Federal regulations provide special protection for patient records in drug- and alcohol-abuse treatment programs funded by the federal government.[17] These include tight restrictions on disclosures from patient records even when a subpoena or court order has been served, and prohibit the use of blanket consent forms. The courts have recognized the special sensitivity of addicts' records. In the best known judicial test of this issue, New York's highest court upheld the refusal of the director of a methadone clinic to give the police photographs of all young black male patients in a murder investigation after a witness claimed to have seen the killer at the clinic. The court's judgment in this case, even where there was an admittedly strong public interest in disclosure, shows an appreciation for the paramount importance of patients' privacy.[18]

But there are equally strong pressures in the other direction. A frequent cause of conflict are the attempts by federal or state officials to inspect patient records in the course of an investigation of a treatment facility for irregularities of practice, or even in a routine service audit. Probation and other court officers often ask for information about patients who have been sent into treatment as an alternative to jail. And, of course, many states and localities, and the federal government itself, maintain addict registries that record extensive personal information, often including names or easily decipherable identifiers, about patients in drug-treatment programs. Many of these registries are available for inspection by a variety of state and federal officials.

The privacy of abortion patients has been viewed with scant sympathy by legislatures and courts. Many state legislatures have enacted mandatory reporting requirements on abortion patients, often in the form of fetal death certificates, bearing the mother's name, that are preserved for inspection by state officials to serve a variety of auditing, evaluation, research, public health, and investigative purposes. Such requirements have been upheld, at least in principle, by the US Supreme Court.[19] In fact even a government computer bank of personally identifiable fetal death certificates survived a constitutional challenge in New York, where the state court of appeals relied on a New York City regulation promising complete confidentiality (except for disclosures to "authorized personnel") of the city's abortion registry as justification for finding no violation of the patients' constitutional right of privacy. One of the court's three dissenters noted the "potential for stigmatization" posed by the existence of such a record system in a society in which abortion is still "an emotionally charged" subject.[20]

A different approach to patient privacy is illustrated by the Multi-State Information System (MSIS), a computerized databank in Rockland County, New York, containing detailed patient diagnostic and treatment records submitted by public and private psychiatric treatment facilities in half a dozen eastern states and the District of Columbia. To protect these records, the New York State legislature enacted a statute in 1972 immunizing MSIS from demands for access to its records by any official or agency, even under subpoena or court order.[21] Of course, the same records may be available to government officials, with or without a court order, in the local facilities at which MSIS records originate, subject to the vagaries of state law.

All fifty states permit minors to receive treatment for venereal disease without parental permission. Many also allow minors to have abortions, contraceptive services, or treatment for drug and alcohol addiction without parental consent. In some states statutes specifically forbid doctors and clinics to disclose such treatment to parents without the child's consent; in others disclosure is allowed at the discretion of the physician.[22]

Despite the development of special legal protection for some kinds of especially sensitive medical records, patients should be aware that these records are in general no more secure than any other medical records. Insurance companies and government service payers can still get them; so can researches, auditors, professional-review committees, welfare agencies, police and other governmental investigators, and even employers. As in so many other instances discussed in this chapter, the degree to which the patient's privacy will be protected depends largely on the alertness, discretion, and resolution of the doctor or hospital administrator who maintains the record.

May a patient sue a doctor or hospital that has made an unauthorized disclosure of medical information?

Yes, but the patient should be warned that such suits rarely succeed. The few that have involved either a disclosure that directly and immediately caused a tangible injury to the patient, such as a loss of employment, or actual publication of medical information, in which case the publisher rather than the doctor was frequently the defendant. A suit for unauthorized disclosure might be formulated on a variety of technical legal grounds: breach of a contractual relationship between doctor and patient in which the doctor's duty to preserve confidentiality is an implied condition of the contract; invasion of privacy; breach of the doctor's fiduciary relationship to the patient; or a broad interpretation of state doctor-patient privilege statutes and laws licensing doctors and psychiatrists[23] If the information disclosed is false, a suit for defamation may be possible. The odds against the patient in all such suits are formidable. A report on medical records published in 1976 by the National Bureau of Standards explains why. First, patients seldom know what disclosures have been made, or where, or to whom. Second, lawsuits require a lot of time and money. Third, and most important, a lawsuit means a public trial, bringing further unwanted publicity that only compounds the damage of the original disclosure. And finally, if past experience is a guide, such a lawsuit is difficult to win.[24]

In nearly half the states, a practitioner can have his or her license revoked for willfully disclosing professional secrets. Confidentiality is an important ethical precept of the medical profession, expressed in the Hippocratic Oath, in the code of ethics of the American Medical Association,[25] and in the codes of many allied health care professions. Nonetheless, although a physician might risk professional or administrative sanctions for improperly disclosing information about a patient, the patient stands only the most remote chance of winning satisfaction or compensation for himself through the courts. In fact, California enacted a law requiring psychiatrists to report dangerous patients to the police. The courts upheld the law in 1983.[26]

For years, privacy advocates have urged state legislatures

and Congress to pass laws giving patients an explicit right of medical confidentiality and a means to enforce that right in the courts. Such statutes, reaching all health care providers and facilities, would have to delineate clearly the permissible conditions for disclosure without patient consent, and provide an effective civil remedy for violations of the patient's expectation of privacy. Until this happens, patient suits for unauthorized disclosures by doctors and hospitals will remain subject to the vagaries of judicial interpretation, which has generally shown greater deference to medical discretion than to patient's expectations.[27] In fact, the House of Representatives nearly approved comprehensive medical privacy legislation in 1980, but the proposal died when lawmakers were unable to resolve a dispute over intelligence agents' access to health files.

Once third parties have obtained medical information from doctors and hospitals, are they legally prevented from making further disclosures?

Only in some circumstances. Medical information received by a federal agency (perhaps in its capacity as a service payer or employer) is protected by the federal Privacy Act of 1974. In general, this means that a disclosure may be made by the agency without the patient's authorization only for "routine uses" compatible with the agency's lawful administrative function, to a law-enforcement agency upon its formal written request or pursuant to a court order.[28]

In states that have privacy laws modeled on the federal Privacy Act, state agencies are similarly restricted in disclosing medical information. Where there is no such state privacy statute, freedom of information or public records laws exempt medical and personnel information from disclosure to the public. Such statutes would not ordinarily, however, prevent state agencies from disclosing medical information to other agencies, or even to certain private organizations, such as insurers or social-services organizations operating under contract to the state. Exempted categories under freedom of information acts do not enjoy special guarantee of confidentiality; they are merely exceptions to an agency's affirmative duty to make records available to the public.

Do patients have a legal right of access to their own medical records?

Because there is no national law covering privately held medical records, the patients' right of access depends on where they live and who is holding the record. For instance, thirteen states provide for patient access to both hospital and doctor records (Alaska, California, Colorado, Connecticut, Georgia, Hawaii, Illinois, Michigan, Minnesota, Nevada, Oklahoma, West Virginia, and Wisconsin).[29] Nine states have provisions for access to hospital records only (Indiana, Maine, Maryland, Massachusetts, Nebraska, Ohio, Pennsylvania, South Dakota, Texas). Two states have a provision for access to doctor files only (Florida, New Jersey).[30] Many states have laws that deal specifically with access to mental health records. Currently, nineteen states and the District of Columbia have statutes that allow patients access to their mental health records (Alaska, Arizona, California, Colorado, Connecticut, Georgia, Hawaii, Illinois, Indiana, Kentucky, Maryland, Michigan, Minnesota, Ohio, Oregon, South Dakota, Virginia, West Virginia, and Wisconsin).[31] The US Constitution does not give a right of access to health files because Supreme Court rulings make the health care provider, not the patient, the owner of the record. On the other hand, all federal health facilities (including VA hospitals) are covered by the Privacy Act, which includes access provisions.

If you live in a state that does not require health care providers to release medical records to patients, do not assume that you will be unable to obtain your records. A survey conducted by the Public Citizens Health Research Group in the District of Columbia, which does not have a patient access law, revealed that nearly 75 percent of the physicians who responded would voluntarily turn over patient's records to the patient if asked.[32]

Do patients have a legal right of access to their own federally held medical records?

The Privacy Act has a separate provision for access to federally held medical files, allowing for "special procedures" that usually permit federal agencies and hospitals to release the record to a physician or health care professional of the patient's choice or to any "responsible person" designated by the individual. The person receiving the records then decides whether to turn them over to the individual. The clumsiness of such "special procedures" is simply a legacy of the diehard attitude that there is danger in a person's knowledge of his own medical and emotional state of health. Oft-mentioned examples are the risks of a revelation of a psychiatric evaluation or terminal illness. In fact few medical records seem to pose such problems. The Privacy Protection Study Commission noted the absence of any witness at the commission's hearing who "was able to identify an instance where access to records has had an untoward effect on a patient's medical condition."[33] In practice, most federal agencies release medical records directly to the individual. The Department of Defense, for example, told the commission that it released records to a physician rather than to the individual directly in less than 1 percent of requests.[34]

Other federal privacy statutes also provide for such indirect access to medical records. The Fair Credit Reporting Act allows credit-reporting agencies to withhold medical information obtained from physicians, hospitals, and other medical personnel and facilities when it informs individuals of the "nature and substance" of the records.[35] The Family Educational Rights and Privacy Act similarly limits students' right to examine and copy medical and psychiatric records maintained by the institution's medical personnel. These records may be released to a physician of the student's choice. The medical records of precollege students under eighteen are released to their parents.[36]

Can employees see medical records held by their employers?

Under Occupational Safety and Health Administration (OSHA) regulations, employees exposed to "toxic substances or harmful physical agents" have a right to see records kept regarding this exposure, whether or not the records are related to specific occupational safety and health hazards. For example, in the case of lead, measurements are taken of concentrations in the air and in workers' blood. Workers are then tested for a wide range of disorders including anemia, brain, nerve, and reproductive damage, kidney impairment, and genetic disorders. The results of these medical tests and the measurements taken of air and blood lead concentrations are now accessible to workers.

The OSHA rule calls for an initial copy to be provided free of cost no later than fifteen days after the request is made and in reasonable place and manner. It also provides for preservation of records for at least thirty years. One purpose of the rule is to encourage more effective worker participation in personal health management.[37]

May a patient correct inaccurate information in a medical record?

Yes, if the incorrect information is in a record held by a person or agency subject to a statute that provides for a right of correction. These include the federal Privacy Act and its state analogs, the Fair Credit Reporting Act, and the Family Educational Rights and Privacy Act. The correction of technical information, such as a diagnosis or the results of a laboratory test, will almost certainly require a submission by a doctor or other professional source. Thus, for example, a person who finds erroneous medical information in her Social Security Administration file will probably have to support her demand for correction, under the federal Privacy Act, with documentation prepared by a qualified professional—a procedure that will often entail more trouble and expense than are required for correction of other kinds of data.

While errors in doctor and hospital records can cause harm, the greater danger lies in errors of medical information contained in third party records, such as those of employers, insurers, and credit-reporting agencies. Where medical information will be used to make nonmedical decisions, it is of the greatest importance for patients to utilize every avenue available to obtain access to the information and its correction or amendment. Patients should not be reluctant to challenge what the record-keepers may assert to be outside the province of the layman. As the Privacy Protection Study Commission wrote, "while it is true that some portion of the information in a medical record may be beyond the patient's comprehension, not all of it will be. . . . [T]he circulation of erroneous, obsolete, incomplete, or irrelevant medical-record information outside the confines of the medical-care relationship can bring substantial harm or embarrassment. . . ." For this reason, the commission recommended the provision of a correction procedure applicable to all medical records and to medical information contained in all third-party nonmedical records.[38]

What kinds of protection exist for records held by insurance companies?

A handful of states, most notably California, Connecticut, and Illinois, have laws granting insurance customers access to their records, limiting insurance companies data collection practices, regulating use of confidentiality waivers, and specifying what disclosures to outsiders are allowable.

These statutes were drafted largely on a model of the National Association of Insurance Commissioners (NAIC), the organization representing state officials who regulate the insurance industry. The NAIC model surfaced in 1979 when Congress was seriously considering national legislation on insurance privacy, pursuant to recommendations of the Privacy Protection Study Commission. The proposal was tougher than the NAIC bill in that it more severely limited disclosures to outsiders, banned pretext interviews, and created a stronger right of consumers' access to their own files. The insurance industry, which has a tradition of enjoying state rather than federal regulation, argued that Congress should wait to see how the states did before departing from tradition and enacting a federal insurance privacy law. The strategy succeeded: the federal proposal died and, as mentioned, less than a dozen states adopted the NAIC model. Thus, in the vast majority of states, customers do not have a legal right of access to their insurance files and cannot expect that insurers will limit disclosures to others.

AIDS has emerged as a highly visible privacy issue in the late 1980s. Why?

Because AIDS is such a deadly disease, information recording who has the disease or who may get it is extremely sensitive. Data indicating that a person was infected, if readily available, could prevent that person from getting a job or getting health or life insurance. Since one must be tested to determine the presence of the AIDS virus, much of the controversy focuses on confidentiality of AIDS test results. Most health officials, gay rights activists, and civil libertarians argue that if complete confidentiality is not guaranteed, then "high risk" groups will shy away from AIDS testing, thus threatening to worsen the problem by failing to inform infected individuals of their condition. There were several significant developments in 1988. As this book goes to press, these are some of the most important:

1. Congress approved $1 billion for AIDS research but withdrew a proposal for new confidentiality protection for AIDS test results because Senator Jesse Helms threatened a filibuster.

2. Separate legal actions were filed in Virginia and New York over alleged violations of confidentiality policies stemming from the disclosure of individuals' AIDS test results. The cases could signal the beginning of a legal counterattack against AIDS-related disclosures, given health officials' prior promises of privacy and the current pressure on them to reveal certain AIDS test results. One case was filed by the mother of a girl whose Virginia county school system allegedly violated the Buckley amendment (protecting school records) by notifying the community that an unnamed student with AIDS soon would be enrolling. The second case arose when a New York City Human Rights Commission lawyer told a hospital agency that it should speed its handling of the case because the victim had AIDS.

3. During its annual meeting in June 1988, the American Medical Association broke with a long tradition of confidentiality and strongly urged physicians to warn the sexual partners of patients found to carry the AIDS virus if there was no other way to alert them to the danger.

4. A state judge in Albany in April 1988 invalidated a New York insurance commission regulation prohibiting insurers from testing for AIDS viruses. Stating that there was no reason to give favored treatment to HIV-infected individuals, Judge Daniel H. Prior, Jr. said that AIDS testing "produces a statistically valid basis for actuarial risk classification purposes as an accurate, significant and substantial predictor of morbidity, mortality and medical expenses."[39]

NOTES

1. The US Supreme Court declined to review a federal appeals court decision upholding an exception in California's privilege statute that allows a psychiatrist to be ordered to testify about a patient if the patient has raised the issue of his own emotional state, such as in a negligence suit. *Ceasar v. Mountanes*, 542 F.2d 1064 (9th Cir., 1976), *cert. denied*, 97 U.S. 1598 (1977).
2. Fed. R. Evid. 501.
3. *Whalen v. Roe*, 429 U.S. 589 (1977).
4. *Privacy Times*, July 24, 1986.
5. *Privacy Times*, July 24, 1986.
6. *Privacy Times*, July 22, 1988.
7. *Privacy Times*, Nov. 8, 1988.
8. Cal. Civ. Code § 56.
9. *Womeldorf (Cox) v. Gleason*, Civ. No. B-75-1086 (D. Md., Nov. 16, 1977).
10. 15 U.S.C. § 1681d.
11. *See, e.g.,* the Social Security Amendments of 1972, Pub. L. No. 92-603, § 249F, establishing professional-standards review organizations for the Medicare, Medicaid, and Maternal and Child Health Programs; 42 U.S.C. § 4582 and 21 U.S.C. § 1175, protecting the confidentiality of patient records in federally funded drug- and alcohol-abuse treatment programs used in research projects; 42 U.S.C. § 242m, governing records obtained by the National Center for Health Statistics.
12. *American Academy of Pediatrics, et al. v. Margaret Heckler*, USDC-D.C. No. 83-0774 (Apr. 14, 1983).
13. *Rasmussen v. South Florida Blood Service*, 500 So. 2d 553 (Fla. 1987).
14. Or. Rev. Stat. § 179.505.
15. 5 U.S.C. § 552a.
16. 45 C.F.R. § 99.31 and 99.36; 5 U.S.C. § 552a(b)(8).
17. 42 C.F.R. § 2.1ff., authorized under 42 U.S.C. § 4582 and 21 U.S.C. § 1175.
18. *People v. Newman*, 32 N.Y.2d 379, 298 N.E.2d 651 (N.Y., 1973).
19. *Planned Parenthood of Central Missouri v. Danforth*, 428 U.S. 52 (1976).
20. *In re Schulman v. New York City Health & Hosp. Corp.*, 379 N.Y.2d 703 (1975).
21. N.Y. Civ. Rights Law § 79(j).
22. *See, e.g.,* Haw. Rev. Stat. § 577A-3 and 4, in which disclosure is mandatory for pregnancy and discretionary for V.D.

23. *Horne v. Patton*, 291 Ala. 701, 287 So. 2d 824 (1973); Note, *Physicians and Surgeons: Civil Liability for a Physician Who Disclosed Medical Information Obtained within the Doctor-Patient Relationship, in a Nonlitigation Setting*, 28 Okla. L. Rev. 3d 658–73 (1975).

24. Alan F. Westin, *Computers, Health Records, and Citizen Rights*, (National Bureau of Standards, Dec. 1976).

25. *Principles of Medical Ethics of the American Medical Association*, 9 (1957).

26. *Privacy Times*, Mar. 30, 83.

27. *See, e.g.*, *Simenson v. Swenson*, 177 S.W. 831 (Neb. 1920), a hotel doctor's disclosure to the landlord that one of the hotel guests had syphilis; *Berry v. Moench*, 331 P.2d 814 (Utah 1958), a doctor's disclosure of psychiatric information about a former patient to the parents of the patient's fiancée; *Clark v. Geraci*, 208 N.Y.S. 2d 564 (Sup. Ct. 1960), a doctor's disclosure to an employer that his patient was an alcoholic; *Hague v. Williams*, 181 A.2d 345 (N.J. 1962), a doctor's disclosure to an insurance company of a baby's congenital heart defect that was unknown to the parents. Note also *Tarasoff v. Regents*, 529 P.2d 553 (Cal. 1974), *aff'd*. rehearing 551 P.2d 334 (Cal. 1976), in which it was held that a psychiatrist has an affirmative duty to warn the intended victim of a violent patient, a decision much criticized for its implications for the right of psychiatric confidentiality.

28. 5 U.S.C. § 552a(b).

29. *Medical Records: Getting Yours*, Pub. Cit. Health Res. Group, (2d ed., 1986).

30. *Id*.

31. *Id*.

32. *Id*.

33. Privacy Protection Study Commission, *supra* note 22, at 297.

34. *Id*.

35. 15 U.S.C. § 1681g(a)(1).

36. 20 U.S.C. § 1232g(a)(4); 45 C.F.R. § 99.3.

37. 28 C.F.R. § 1910.20.

38. Privacy Protection Study Commission, *supra* note 22, at 300.

39. *In the Matter of the Application of Health Insurance Association of America et al. v. James P. Corcoran*, N.Y. Sup. Ct., Albany; No. 01-87-St, 1078; Apr. 16, 1988.

XIII
Viewing and Reading Records

The books you read, as well as the movies and television shows that you watch, reflect personal choices that can reveal political or religious beliefs, sexual preferences, or other personal matters that should not be made known to strangers without your consent. More and more, viewing and reading habits are recorded electronically by video rental stores, pay television services, and libraries. This growing body of records illustrates the increasing intersection of First Amendment interests in free speech and association with Fourth Amendment interests in privacy. In recent years, lawmakers have responded with strict disclosure standards to protect the privacy of these records.

What is the purpose of the Video Privacy Protection Act of 1988?

The law establishes new confidentiality safeguards for records kept by video rental stores (and others who provide videos) on what movies their customers take home. The provisions enable customers whose records are disclosed without their consent to sue for damages of up to $4,000.

Are law enforcers able to obtain these records?

To obtain records under the statute, law enforcement officials must secure a court order by showing that there is "clear and convincing evidence that the subject of the information sought would be material evidence in the case." Further, the law gives an individual an opportunity to challenge the court order before records are disclosed. The "clear and convincing standard," the strongest one regulating law enforcement access to privately held files, is patterned after the confidentiality provisions of the 1984 Cable Communication Policy Act.

Does the law bar the use of customer lists held by video rental stores for marketing purposes?

Not exactly. It requires the video provider to offer customers a clearly explained choice of whether they want their names and addresses released for marketing purposes. Even if customers consent to disclosure of their names and addresses the law still prohibits the release of files showing what specific videos they rent, unless they give their consent.

What prompted Congress to pass the law?

During the Senate hearings on the nomination of Robert Bork to the Supreme Court, a reporter for Washington's *City Paper* was in a video store when an employee mentioned to him that Bork rented videos there as well. The reporter asked if the employee could give him records showing what movies Bork had selected. The employee handed over the material, and the reporter published an article supposedly describing Bork's viewing habits. (Of course it was possible that Bork's family members, or even out-of-town visitors, actually had checked out some or all of the movies shown by the records.) The story sparked protests from Bork's supporters and opponents alike.

The first legislator to propose new legal safeguards was Representative Al McCandless (R-CA). He was joined by Representative Robert Kastenmeier (D-WI) and, in the Senate, Senators Patrick Leahy (D-VT), Paul Simon (D-IL), Alan Simpson (R-WY),and Charles Grassley (R-IA), who introduced legislation to protect not only video files, but library records as well.

Why were library records included in this effort?

In 1987, stories began surfacing that the FBI, as part of a foreign counterintelligence program, was asking employees at certain technical, university, and public libraries to watch out for foreign spies who were seeking to piece together important scientific and technological data. FBI agents often bypassed head librarians to ask library employees to spot people with foreign sounding names or accents. In a few cases, FBI agents asked to see records showing what books library users had checked out. The requests clashed with the American Library Association's strong code of ethics for library confidentiality, as well as safeguards embodied in thirty-six state laws. The Senate bill attempted to make these widely accepted policies federal law. The FBI lobbied hard and successfully against including the library provisions in the video privacy bill without an exemption for FBI access. The outcome was that the video privacy bill did not address the library issue at all.

What about the thirty-six state laws that cover library records?

Basically, they bar disclosure of library user files without the user's consent. Most require police and other outsiders to meet a tough standard to get a court to order disclosure.

Are the cable television law's privacy provisions similar to the video statute?

Yes. A government entity may obtain personally identifiable data on a cable subscriber only when it "offers clear and convincing evidence that the subject of the information is reasonably suspected of engaging in criminal activity and that the information sought would be material evidence in the case (and) the subject of the information is afforded the opportunity to appear and contest such entity's claim."

A subscriber can bring a suit for wrongful disclosure for actual damages of at least $1,000, punitive damages, and reasonable attorney's fees. Cable companies must fully inform subscribers of their rights, which include the right to see all data held on them by cable companies and to correct any erroneous data. Cable firms are required to destroy personal data when keeping them is "no longer necessary for the purpose for which they were collected."

XIV

The Wild Card: Private Detectives

What is a private detective?

A private detective is someone who, for a fee, investigates people, businesses, or cases for private clients. They are also known as private investigators. In most cases they are former police or intelligence officers.

How many private investigators are there?

One estimate puts the number at 65,000.[1] The price for a private investigator's services can range from $45 a day to $1,000 a day, depending, of course, on the experience and reputation of the investigator, the job at hand, and the client. Private investigating is a multimillion dollar business in the United States. Increasingly, law firms are turning to private investigators to cut prelitigation costs. In 1988, many investigators reported 25 percent annual growth in their law firm business.

Is the old image of private detectives still valid — Sam Spade-type men in dirty overcoats watching a front door all night from a parked car?

Generally not. In recent years there has been a fundamental shift in which private detectives less and less have to "tail" people and instead find out what they need by searching through databases. In other words, they are benefiting from the advent of a computerized "information society" that allows those who are "plugged into" key computers to engage in data surveillance.

What kind of data can private investigators gain access to?

All kinds, and that's the point. An informal survey of a representative sample of private investigators confirmed what most people already believe to be the case: private investigators can find almost any information they want, regardless of privacy laws or any other security measures. One private investigator, who asks that his name be withheld, said, "If there's enough money you can get anything. You have to find the weak link in the chain and go for it!" "I've never heard of a record I couldn't get if I put my mind to it," said another investigator who also requests anonymity.

In fact, no investigator interviewed seemed troubled about disclosure restrictions imposed by various privacy laws. They described why no record was virtually beyond their reach; "It's all based on contacts," explained one investigator who has experience in federal law enforcement and congressional and private sector security. He added, "Law enforcement officials and former law enforcers who become private investigators form a loose-knit fraternity. Those with a law enforcement background have instant credibility. Federal agents usually have contacts at the state level, who, in turn, have contacts at the local level. . . . Private eyes working outside their network must find a colleague to refer him to the proper source — usually another private investigator — and then 'subcontract' with him to get the information you need."

When investigators can't get confidential data through their network of contacts, they must resort to more imaginative methods. This includes going through the garbage to get important records or to obtaining computer passwords that enable an outsider to tap into a databank via the telephone.

Ernie Rizzo, a Chicago private eye, once drugged a Doberman pinscher with tainted meat in order to sift through the owner's garbage for financial records.[2] Rizzo, a flamboyant detective who tackles high profile cases and brags to the press about his escapades, said on another assignment he was told to find out if Bing Crosby was about to retire. Rizzo proudly related that he intercepted Western Union telegrams from the family confirming the impending retirement by checking into the Beverly Hilton under the name Gary Crosby.

Rizzo once had to investigate a man filing for bankruptcy who claimed he had no assets and could not afford his own place and lived with a relative. Rizzo learned the man owned several small stores in faraway cities, went to one of them, and purchased items with a personal check. When the checks cleared he learned what bank the man used, and obtained confidential bank records which showed the man owned and lived in an expensive home.

Switzerland is famous for its bank secrecy laws, but an investigator said he was able to obtain Swiss bank records that were crucial to a case on which he was working. "It's the same with the Cayman Islands and Panama," the investigator said, referring to other countries with supposedly strict bank secrecy laws. "You can get them. You just have to work a little harder."

Medical records are now more difficult to get, investigators said. That wasn't always the case. In the 1970s, a scandal surfaced in Colorado after private investigators and insurance companies used false identities to obtain confidential health files from hospitals. The culprits were prosecuted, but the state supreme court said they could not be tried under theft laws because "information was not a thing of value."[3] In Ontario, Canada a provincial commission found that private investigators assumed identities, and insurance company-paid physicians went through hospital records and divulged private data.[4] An unnamed investigator told Newsweek magazine in 1974 that he had "friends in hospitals who will steal records for him and another friend who has a truck for making keys on-site."[5] The present situation in the United States is apparently changed. "The Medical Information Bureau is tougher to tap into," confided one private eye. "Medical records are harder to get. We only get them through our 'contact,' and that is only verbally," said the head of another major detective agency. He did not elaborate on what—or who—his contact was.

Private investigators also obtain private records by posing as repairmen, telephone company officials, delivery personnel, and other occupations that visit offices routinely.

Don't private eyes ever get caught illegally obtaining personal data?

Seldom. In addition to the Colorado and Ontario cases from the 1970s cited above, there was one instance in which four detectives in a St. Louis firm pleaded guilty for violating the federal Privacy Act which prohibits people from obtaining confidential records under false pretenses. Court records showed that St. Louis area police departments regularly secured records from the FBI's National Crime Information Center and then sold them to Fitzgerald & Dorsey. Robert

Dorsey, who pleaded guilty to four violations of the Privacy Act, was fined $10,000. Fines for the police officers involved ranged from $800 to $3,000.[6] The case arose when Pat Clawson, at the time an employee of Fitzgerald & Dorsey, blew the whistle on the record trafficking operation. A subsequent search found various logs indicating that some police officers kept track of each record sold to the private eye firm for billing purposes, while other officers had more of a monthly "retainer" arrangement.[7]

But don't private detectives spend a lot of their time obtaining personal information legally?

Of course. But due to the explosion of both general and specialized databanks that now make easily accessible what was previously hard to get personal information, the implications for personal privacy are just as serious. Because modern technology permits people to search different databases, computers allow access to private tax records, telephone bills, and health information once difficult or impossible to obtain legally. Now an investigator can search through thousands of court cases, motor vehicle and property electronic files, and obscure filings to find a tax return produced in a business or divorce case in which personal assets are at issue. Moreover, service companies have turned tidy profits creating computer banks of sensitive, personal data that investigative firms can subscribe to. "They offered the first one for private detectives about 1983, now there are hundreds," said Nicholas R. Bertrande, head of a Washington firm. Bertrande added that his firm, like many of the large private detective companies, are creating their own, customized databanks. Bertrande's company already has four customized databanks covering real estate, financial, and other economic data.

Some civil libertarians fret over the future of information privacy. "There are important questions about someone punching keys on a computer making unalterable decisions about a person's life," said Richard D. Emery, a civil liberties lawyer in Manhattan.[8]

"Information is power," said Vincent Parco, who heads a Manhattan investigative firm. "The more information you have, the more power you have in court."[9] That seems to be the bottom line for all too many.

NOTES

1. *New York Times*, July 15, 1988.
2. *The Sunday Herald*, Apr. 20, 1980.
3. Access Reports/Privacy, Mar. 1979.
4. Govt. of Ontario, *Investigation of the Royal Commission on Medical Records* (1979).
5. *Newsweek*, Mar. 21, 1974, vol. 1, no. 50.
6. *Privacy Times*, Oct. 6, 1982.
7. *Id.*
8. *New York Times*, July 15, 1988.
9. *Id.*

Appendix A
Sample Request Letter

Your address
Your telephone no.
Date

Director
United States Agency
Washington, D.C.

Dear Madam/Sir:

This is a request under the Freedom of Information Act (5 U.S.C. 552) and the Privacy Act (5 U.S.C. 552a). I request a copy of [describe your request; for example, "all documents maintained by your agency about me"].

In the event that you determine that some portion of a file is exempt from release, I request that you release any reasonably segregable portion of the documents which is not exempt. I, of course, reserve my right to appeal such decisions.

In addition, if you determine that some or all of the report is exempt, I request that you advise me of the applicable exemption and explain why it applies in this case.

As you know, the law permits you to waive or reduce fees if this is "in the public interest because furnishing the information can be considered as primarily benefitting the public." I believe that this request fits that category and ask you to waive any fees.

If you have any questions regarding this request, please feel free to contact me.

Sincerely,

Your name

Appendix B
Sample Letter of Appeal

Your address
Your telephone no.
Date

Secretary of Department
United States Department
Washington, D.C.

Dear Madam/Sir:

This is an appeal pursuant to the Freedom of Information Act (5 U.S.C. 552).

On _____ I received a letter from _____ of your department advising me that my request for access to documents has been denied in part. I am enclosing a copy of my exchange of correspondence with your agency so that you can see what files I have requested and that the request has been denied.

I trust that upon examination of my request you will conclude that the information sought is not properly covered by the exemptions cited. I expect that you will make such information available promptly.

If you are unable to order release of the requested information, I intend to initiate a lawsuit to compel its disclosure.

Sincerely,

Your name